CATCHING UP WITH JESUS

Some scholars like to explore the Jewishness of Jesus, while others opt for the Cosmic Christ. The one belongs to the realm of history, the other to the horizons of archetypal meaning. The former is local and historically grounded, the latter, global, transcending time and space.

Both strands belong to the Jesus story, giving it an enduring fascination. How we integrate the two dimensions is a new challenge for our time, as growing numbers of Christians embrace larger horizons in their search for spiritual, human, and earthly meaning.

This book is an attempt at a contemporary Jesus story for Christians and others who engage with the new cosmology and explore new scientific insights arising from quantum physics. The Jesus contained within strict historical boundaries finds little space in this new worldview, while the Jesus who launched a daring new world, described in the Gospels as the Kingdom of God, very much belongs here.

Those excited by the new story of creation and science need not abandon their Christian faith as something archaic and irrelevant. Quite the contrary, Christian faith itself can illuminate these new horizons, but we need to access the Jesus story with fresh imagination and a relevant, invigorating narrative. Then Christian faith and science can embrace a fruitful and liberating partnership.

DIARMUID O'MURCHU is a social psychologist and a member of a Catholic Religious Order. As a lifelong learner, he embraces a multidisciplinary approach, based on work in Europe, the United States, Asia, Australia, and Africa. His written works include *Reclaiming Spirituality, Religion in Exile, Quantum Theology* (all published by Crossroad), and *Evolutionary Faith* (published by Orbis Books).

Catching Up with Jesus

A Gospel Story for Our Time

DIARMUID O'MURCHU MSC
(Author of *Quantum Theology*)

The Crossroad Publishing Company
New York

The Crossroad Publishing Company
481 Eighth Avenue, Suite 1550, New York, NY 10001

This book is set in 11/14 Sabon.
The display type is Tiepolo Book.

Printed in the United States of America

Library of Congress Cataloging-in-Publication Data

Ó Murchú, Diarmuid.
    Catching up with Jesus : a gospel story for our time / Diarmuid O'Murchu.
        p. cm.
    Includes bibliographical references.
    ISBN 0-8245-2298-2 (alk. paper)
    1. Jesus Christ. 2. Jesus Christ—Person and offices. 3. Quantum theory. 4. Evolution—Religious aspects—Christianity. I. Title.
BT304.9.O48 2005
232—dc22

                                                                2005003090

4   5   6   7   8   9   10   09   08   07   06

Contents

Introduction

FOR SEVERAL YEARS NOW, people have been asking me about the place of Jesus in the newly emerging worldview of our time. The request tends to take three different but overlapping forms:

- Is there a place for Jesus in the new cosmology?
- What might christology look like in the context of Quantum Theology?
- How do we reappropriate our Christian faith in the context of the big story of evolution?

These are profound theological questions not easily addressed within the specific world of Christian theology. They stretch all our conventional paradigms in terms of both faith and our understanding of the world we inhabit. I suspect that the questions can be addressed only from a multidisciplinary perspective. And I am not at all sure that the questions can be answered in the sense of providing a neat conceptual response. The wisdom may be in the questions themselves rather than in any answer that scholarship might try to provide.

Formidable though the questions are, it is obvious that millions around our world are grappling with them and seek an intelligent response. From a Christian viewpoint, those seeking new truth tend not to be regular churchgoers, on the one hand, nor formal theologians, on the other. They are an in-between group, familiar with the Christian story but suspicious that the churches do not unpack it—nor live it out—in a creative or liberating way.

For well over ten years now, I have journeyed with such people, heard their stories, and engaged with their questions. As a social scientist, I feel privileged to have won the trust of those who pose the questions and blessed with a bigger picture of reality to be able to contextualize the questions in a new way. I do not consider this to be a superior position, spiritually, humanly, or otherwise. It is a grassroots perspective that formal scholarship tends to ignore or bypass. Ideally, I would like to think of it as a complementary set of insights to those of the scholarly world. I say "ideally" because my experience suggests that the scholarly world is not very open to these ideas and at times exhibits a distinct hostility to those of us who try to express them.

From a scholarly perspective, the Jesus story is for scripture scholars, theologians, or people immersed in the spiritual life. Formally, I belong to none of those categories, and neither do the people who have inspired and challenged me to write this book. Jesus belongs to all of us who have struggled with faith, as well as grown through it, who question it as much as abide by its guidelines. For many people on the periphery, or perhaps beyond it, Jesus is an archetypal figure with an enduring fascination. I have agnostic and atheistic friends who live out of a set of values far more congruent with the Gospels (it seems to me) than some practicing Christians do.

There is something about Jesus that is bigger and more engaging than the formalized Christian story. Jesus grips the creative imagination to a degree that makes Christian dogma look insipid and reductionistic. The Jesus story awakens meaning in the human soul, and this requires a fresh engagement with the living story as distinct from the fixed dogmas.

This book consists mainly of a story. It is the Jesus story told by an imaginary Jesus of our time. It is a story that incorporates some of the well-known facts of the inherited tradition but stretches the meaning of the facts in the direction of the contemporary imagination. Jesus was very much a prophet of the creative imagination, demolishing boundaries and inviting people to radically new horizons of vision and fresh hope.

The book is written primarily for spiritual seekers of a Christian culture or background. It is designed for *adult* learners who can trust intuition, take risks, and have their horizons of understanding continually stretched. Respecting the *adult* in each reader, I have not adopted arguments to justify or defend the approach I use; that can be explored later, honoring the principle that in the sphere of adult education we learn primarily from experience and from the mutual dialogue arising from that experience.

My hope is that this book, in however small a way, will open up horizons of hope and fresh meaning for the questioning people of our time.

1

Bringing Jesus out of Captivity

Christianity has fossilized a powerful story. . . . The list of Christologies of oppression is long.

—Lisa Isherwood

"SET MY PEOPLE FREE" is the clarion call of the Christian Gospel. The Jesus who came that we might have life and have it to the full (John 10:10) has often become the victim of those forces that diminish the meaning and potential of life. Before we can hope to reclaim a more liberating version of the Jesus story, we need to prune the prevailing story of the accretions of time and the calcifications of culture. We need to allow the real Jesus to be real once more.

The Jesus story defies all our efforts at comprehensiveness. It breaks through the particular renditions of each new generation. Assuredly there are enduring elements, and perhaps things that never change. But our understanding changes. Indeed, it needs to change continuously, otherwise we fall foul of ideology and idolatry.

Jesus, too, has been made the object of ideological reductionism. He has been imprisoned in the ideologies of human power and domination, and that same destructive process is likely to continue until the forces of captivity are named and exposed. That I hope to do—in a small way—in the opening chapter of this book.

My approach is similar to that of the feminist scholar Anne Clifford (2001), whose theological reflection unfolds around the primary tasks of *criticism, recovery,* and *reconstruction.* For much of the twentieth century, scholars cleared away the cultural debris that had accumulated around the story of Jesus. They offered critical analyses even of his religious context and the religious attributions devised in the name of Christendom. But there is one aspect that still awaits major redress: *the culture of patriarchy*—the largely male, imperial, rational monopoly on how Jesus should be understood, worshiped, and honored. That is the final bastion that still has to be overthrown. I hope the present work is one small step toward that long-awaited goal.

As we move beyond the constrictions of patriarchal domination, we begin to glimpse a larger landscape that patriarchy never allowed us to consider, the archetypal realm that is foundational and preexistent to the historical Jesus. This is the landscape where Jesus can really be Jesus and where our faith in Jesus is stretched toward new and inspiring horizons (as I briefly review in chapter 2). Several contemporary scholars are moving the Jesus story in this direction.[1] This is the beginning of the process of *recovery,* leading inevitably into the phase of *reconstruction.*

As a social scientist, I like to reconstruct around generic questions rather than with well-worn, conventional answers. In the complex world of our time, engaging with the right questions tends to be the secret to unlocking possibilities. Predictable answers carry diminished significance for our time. In the Jesus story, the question I like to return to time and again is: *"Who do you say that I am?"* (Mk. 8:29). From the Christian point of view I suggest that this is the most important question that has ever been asked, and Christianity is likely to remain well on course while we keep asking it. The day we offer a dogmatic answer we will have capitulated to the rule of idolatry.

The *reconstruction* of the Jesus story in chapter 3 of this book is envisioned around that great question of identity. Jesus never answers the question, but uses it as a catalyst whereby we humans, individually and collectively, are invited to question ourselves and our role in God's world at each new cultural moment. There are no specific conclusions, but there is a story—ever old and ever new—and we are its narrators today. The word continues to become flesh in these questing and questioning times.

As I begin to engage with this material, a statement of Desmond Tutu of South Africa springs to mind: "We don't want our chains loosened; we want them removed!" The chain that binds and incarcerates is the metaphor I wish to adopt for the considerations of this opening chapter—as I review twelve forms of captivity that we have imposed on Jesus throughout the two thousand years of Christendom.

FIRST CHAIN

The Captivity of the Two Thousand Years of Incarnational Reductionism

> The question about the truth of the Christian message has to do with whether it can still disclose to us today the unity of the reality in which we live.
>
> —*Wolfhart Pannenberg*

> That God cannot be embodied except, for example, in the ecclesiastically controlled, historical event of an individual man from Nazareth is hubris of the highest degree.
>
> —*Laurel C. Schneider*

CHRISTIANS BELIEVE THAT GOD has been at work in creation since the dawn of time. There never has been a time when God was not fully involved. The creation account in the Book of Genesis indicates God's pleasure with the creative process. Everything is good, because everything is of God.

Now if God is fully at work at every stage of the evolutionary process, presumably this includes the first emergence of the human species, about six million years ago.[2] Around that time we broke loose from our primate ancestors and became a species in our own right. Divine creativity had added a new dimension to the diversity and elegance of creation.

One does not need to be either a paleontologist or a theologian to appreciate the significance of that moment. It was another quantum leap in the evolutionary story of creation. It was another manifestation and confirmation of divine creativity, bestowed with the typical proclivity and abundance with which the divine life force cocreates.

Incarnation

It happened six million years ago! Assuming that God was totally present to that unfolding and affirming its unique emergence, then, strictly speaking, that is where the incarnation of God in our species happens for the first time. Incarnation basically means God entering fully and identifying with human embodiment.[3] God did that in our species for the first time six million years ago. Unambiguously, without reserve or regret, the divine became manifest in creation in a totally new way, namely, in human form.

Incarnation, as a Christian concept, does not begin two thousand years ago with Jesus of Nazareth. It begins six million years ago, when humans evolved for the first time. The God who totally affirmed our humanity six million years ago was not looking down the evolutionary line and musing: "I'm creating these creatures now, but then I will wait for about six million years until Jesus of Nazareth comes to earth, and only then will I declare them saved." The very argument sounds distorted, convoluted, and ridiculous. Yet, that line of argument forms the basic assumption of the Christian faith over the two thousand years of Christendom.

Contemporary global civilization—Christian and non-Christian alike—uses the two-thousand-year benchmark as a cultural watershed. We use it as a starting point from which so much else follows. Christians extensively regard it as the date before which nothing of consequence prevailed. This is a form of reductionism with stultifying effects of terrifying proportion. Contrary to the widely accepted perception, it is a shriveled, menial understanding that seriously undermines the grandeur of God and the elegance of humanity's story.

As a benchmark, extensively adopted in every field of human learning, it heavily endorses the patriarchal will to dominate and control. That which has unfolded over the past two thousand years we can subject to our scrutiny and management. We can mold and fashion it to our anthropocentric satisfaction. We can create reality to serve our ends and purposes as the self-appointed rulers of the rest of creation.

Then in a kind of bizarre (ir)rational twist, we postulate the God of Christianity as the one who validates our desire for dominance, totally oblivious, it seems, to the Jesus we have actually constructed in our own image and likeness. From a Christian perspective, what we first subjected to our control and management was the person of Jesus himself—his story, his vision, and his radical dream for the renewal of humanity.

Jesus and the Creation Story

Any attempt to bring Jesus out of captivity needs to begin from the basis of creation at large.[4] We are just one of billions of species that inhabit the planet, assuredly unique and special but not with a divine (or human) right to conquer and control all before us. Our insatiable whim for dominance can be seen for what it really is when we adopt the larger context of creation to which we belong. In fact, all we need do is to honor the unfolding story of our own evolution over the time span of the six million years.

The incarnational revelation of our God belongs primarily to the six-million-year cycle. Jesus of Nazareth marks not the beginning of some unique divine enterprise but rather *its fulfillment*. The Jesus story is about an end point, not a starting point. The revelation of God in Jesus is a celebration and affirmation of everything we humans achieved in our six-million-year story. Perhaps, this is what Richard Rohr (2004, 118) has in mind when he writes: "We are all part of a great parade about which we know little, it seems. The essential gospel has not been proclaimed very well. We prefer to doubt both Jesus' incarnation and our own. It is, frankly, just too much."

The Jesuit priest and paleontologist Pierre Teilhard de Chardin is one of the few people who seem to have grasped the larger context. Writing in the early part of the twentieth century, he discerned that our biological human evolution was close to completion. Biologically and physically, we could not evolve much further. In the biological dimension of our existence God has achieved what God set out to achieve. The coming of God among us in the biological embodiment of Jesus was a radical affirmation of that achievement.

But Jesus was more than a biologically embodied creature. His presence was also characterized by several transpersonal capacities, all too easily explained away by divine attribution. Jesus also represented the transbiological state into which humans would now begin to evolve. Teilhard calls this "psychic evolution."[5] It would be characterized primarily by the acquisition and development of new powers of mind and spirit. The epitome of this new humanity is what Christians call the resurrected Christ.

The coming of Jesus in our spiritualized human story marks two moments in what Grace Jantzen (1998) calls the process of *natility* (translated as "becoming" or "flourishing"). The first moment was, and is, one of affirmation—more accurately, confirmation—of all that humans had achieved as cocreators with God over the six-million-year period. The second moment is marked by a new evolutionary threshold indicating the way forward for future human growth and development, primarily in the realm of mind and spirit.

I suggest we view the past two thousand years, creatively understood, as a liminal space, an in-between time, marking a new moment of departure for our species in the invitation once more to become cocreators with our creative God. *It has taken us two thousand years to catch up with Jesus* and to wake up to what is really going on for us as a Christian people. To our narrow functional minds, two thousand years seems a long time. In the evolutionary time scale—which is God's perspective on time—it is merely a few passing seconds!

Now that we are waking up, we face big adjustments. The patriarchal culture of control and reductionism is beginning to wear thin. It no longer inspires and correspondingly, no longer controls. As a species we are emerging out of captivity and beginning to face the disturbing realization that not only were we held captive by the shackles of patriarchy but so was our God. And to make the arrangement respectable and marketable we baptized and ratified it as the Christian church.

"Set my people free" still resounds across the suffering and oppressed world of Christian women and men. It is the clarion call of Jesus to all who are deprived of that fullness of human potential illustrated graphically in our human evolutionary story. But how can the people be free while their God is held captive? Now that we can liberate Jesus from the reductionistic bondage of the past two thousand years, there is renewed hope and promise for those who yearn for true and enduring freedom.

SECOND CHAIN

From the Captivity of Divine Supremacy

> So the Church perpetually teaches the achieved union of divinity and humanity in Christ, and perpetually must fail to deliver what it promises. The promise that the two worlds are now united is maintained by an institution that must insist on keeping them distinct. Christ is caught here in an awkward double-bind that must embarrass him greatly.
>
> —*Don Cupitt*

BY REDUCING OUR HUMAN STORY to the congested context of a mere two thousand years, we inevitably distort God's role in that story. Human projections play themselves out creating several false idols. In our desire to protect the primacy of the divine, we begin to envisage the divine in a way that will validate and justify our human desire for absolute power. In our desire for absolute clarity on the interrelating of the divine (the doctrine of the Trinity), we fail to confront the oppressive and destructive relating among humans, often validated by patriarchal religion.

In striving to give prior attention to the divinity of Jesus, we have caricatured his humanity in a way that seriously compromises the divine potential of the human itself. Like the apostles, we have consistently tried to put Jesus on a divine pedestal—thus avoiding the challenge of a radically new way of being human. Unconsciously for the greater part, we seem to focus on the divine prerogative because it justifies our human desire for absolute power. One wonders if this was not the primary agenda behind the christological doctrines of Nicaea and Chalcedon!

From Power to Trust

I suggest we ask ourselves the question, Why are we, humans, so preoccupied with the divinity of Jesus? We assume that such a preoccupation enhances our growth in faith and reinforces our meaning in life. At best we achieve these goals in a partial way with a distinctive focus beyond this life rather than within it. The realm of the divine is projected into that eternal, perfect realm beyond the precarious and unreliable creation of our daily experience.

Is that what Jesus wanted to achieve through his life witness? Was the salvation of the immortal soul his primary concern? According to John's Gospel, Jesus' union with the Father in exalted glory seems to be a central theme, but we need to ask how much of that concern belongs to Jesus and how much belongs to the theologian(s) who compiled the Fourth Gospel.

Already in the Synoptic Gospels we detect a consistent movement to interpret Jesus as an exalted divine figure. In the culture of Roman oppression and religious millenarian hope, the promise of a divine liberator exerts a powerful appeal. But was it to the fore in the mind of Jesus? Yes, he promised liberation and new life! For the disciples on the road to Emmaus (Luke 24:13ff.) this primarily meant setting Israel free from foreign occupation. Was that the freedom Jesus promised, or was it a great deal more than that?

Where Does the Emphasis Rest?

Scripture scholar Robert Funk (1996) makes an intriguing observation. He devoted over thirty years of his life to the exploration and teaching of scripture, lecturing extensively in United States and Canada. On innumerable occasions he was asked if he believed in the divinity of Jesus; his hearers seemed unsure whether he did or not and often asked him publicly about it. But never once—in over thirty years—was he asked if he believed in the *humanity* of Jesus.

Here, I suggest, we touch on the crucible of Christian faith. It seems to me, that in espousing the Kingdom of God as the central focus of his life and ministry, Jesus was offering a radically new way of *being human*. It was a relational understanding fundamentally different from the patriarchal approach characterized by power and domination. There is ample evidence in the Gospels that the first followers, especially the twelve, were unable to comprehend or grasp this core truth in the Jesus story. The preoccupation with messiahship and exalted glory became major obstacles to seeing the deeper truth of what Jesus was about.

By locating Jesus in the reductionistic context of linear time, the early Christians failed to grasp the liberative vision of the Christ of deep time, the Jesus who was marking and celebrating the fulfillment of six million years of divine creativity in the human species. The early Christians were ignorant of the great human story and consequently were unable to comprehend the human face of God revealed through that story, reaching an evolutionary apex in the life and ministry of Jesus.

By relishing that great story and discerning God's grace and creativity at work in it, we have a more credible and authentic doorway to the divinity of Jesus. And we also begin to realize that the divinity of Jesus is not the primary concern for us, but rather the radically new way of being human, the program of the Kingdom of God, for which Jesus is the primary disciple.

The divine superiority we attribute to Jesus, the understanding we painstakingly honor in worship and doctrine, may well be a major obstacle to a true following of Jesus as the Christ of faith. We condemn Jesus to divine captivity, thus obfuscating both his divinity and his humanity. In the exalted pedestal of patriarchal projection, Jesus is so divinely holy and remote that his radically new way of being human ends up in jeopardy and is seriously compromised. The power of his message is domesticated, the challenge is muted, and the glory of God fully alive in the human is overshadowed by the addictive hunger for divine power and glory. Our preoccupation with the divinity of Jesus may well be a gross distraction from really knowing who Jesus is.

Third Chain

The Captivity of Academic Rationality

> Academics are dominated by intellectual orthodoxies that are self-perpetuating. Professional scholars tyrannize their students and each other. If you want to think new thoughts go out into the wilderness.
> —*S. Warren Carey*

> It's the best possible time to be alive, when almost everything you thought you knew is wrong.
> —*Tom Stoppard*

I N THE *NICOMACHEAN ETHICS,* Aristotle declares the power of reason to be the primary feature of human nature. In other words, we discover truth through the rational mind. We reason our way into reality by thinking clearly and rationally. Imagination and intuition are suspect, and storytelling is for those not sufficiently advanced to deal with the hard factual realities of life.

The Rational Jesus

A great deal of Christian rhetoric condemns Jesus into being a good rationalist. We fit him into the prevailing system of domination, tracing his progeny to a royal male line (Matt. 1:1–17) and proffer his patriarchal status as the firstborn male in a conventional Jewish family. Our inherited christology depicts Jesus as basically a loyal and faithful Jew, although closer examination of the sources clearly shows major divergence from that faith system. His obedience to the ruling Father God—even to the point of death—has been used to exonerate systems of oppressive governance within and outside Christian churches. And the following of Christ has been postulated on rational allegiance and fidelity to divinely sanctioned laws and regulations.

Although Jesus has also been the fascination of prophets and sages, poets and mystics, artists and dramatists, rarely have we taken seriously their narrative portrayals. Those renditions which depict Jesus as a creative rebel, a passionate justice-maker, a visionary of the prophetic imagination are too ambitious and "wild" for the world of rational rhetoric. The dominant culture could not contain, manage, or control this creative dreamer. So, we confine him to the cult of rational discourse attributing dogmatic certainty to those elements we could establish with rational argument and logical deduction.

The Jesus story came to be known as a set of facts around which his life was written and explained, a set of truths decreed by male ecclesiastics, a set of requirements indicating who can be "in" and who must remain "out." As far as possible Jesus was restrained by a culture of respectability, a movement that began in his earthly lifetime and culminated in his being declared the Pantocrator, Constantine's ruler of the universe. The triumph of rationalism was now assured and would control the Christian story for the next seventeen hundred years.

Retrieving the Story

Rational discourse does not feature strongly in the life or mission of Jesus. He told stories, some of which were shocking and all of which were mind-stretching. He transgressed the boundaries that incapacitated the poor and marginalized, and the new liberation became the basis of several miracle stories. He defied convention—religious, social, and political. Perhaps most outrageous of all, he flaunted the sacred hopes of established order, calling forth a new form of governance based on radical equality and inclusivity.

Stories are of central importance in our desire to access the real Jesus. Several contemporary scholars endorse this conviction. But few follow through the inherent logic of that insight, proposing as Nicola Slee does, that *parable* might also be the most generic literary device to unravel the life of Jesus. Slee (in Hampson 1996, 42, 47) writes:

> Like the parables the Jesus story is told with a marked economy and vividness of description and evocation, allied with an absence of explanation or interpretation, such that it is the story itself that holds

the meaning and the reader is constantly teased into making his or her judgement about it. Like the parables it is a story characterised by elements of shock, surprise, extravagance and reversal which disrupts the horizons of normalcy and compels the reader to come to decision and judgement. And like the parables, it is a story that is open to multiple interpretation, thus respecting both the freedom and creative imagination of every reader. . . . [The story of Jesus] disallows slavish imitation or mere repetition and compels the hearer to take responsibility for its narrative development in her own life and times; the story provides a framework of shared beginnings which can only be completed in the hearers own words and ways. And like the parable, it refuses every attempt at final closure.

Rational discourse works in a series of discrete stages; the strategy of storytelling, somewhat like the nature of light in quantum physics, explodes in creative outbursts of energy. Rational discourse assumes a giver and a receiver, a teacher and a learner; storytelling is a mutually enriching interaction between teller and listener. Rational discourse seeks to break things down into constituent parts; storytelling invokes the principle that the whole is greater than the sum of the parts. Rational discourse tends to draw on past traditions and what is known to work; storytelling dreams worlds of alternative possibilities. In rational discourse there is a clear point of ending; good stories always leave possibilities wide open.[6]

We associate storytelling with children, and perhaps that has been a subconscious attempt to subvert the power of storytelling. We forget that adults, too, love telling stories and often do so in order to communicate experiential knowledge through the narrative approach. Storytelling, or more accurately, story-sharing, is a powerful means for calling forth the adult in others. Dare we suggest that that was the primary reason why Jesus (and many of the other great religious leaders) used the medium of story to impart profound truths. Not only was it predominantly an oral culture, but that precise propensity for oral articulation is what humans had known for thousands of years in their engagement with life, creation, and the divine.

Rational discourse delights in facts and in isolating the proof for what works and what doesn't work. Storytelling rejoices in the world of creation, evolution, imagination, and process. While the former is about containment, the latter is about expansiveness.

Rationalism sets boundaries within which control can be exercised, but storytelling opens up horizons that lure us on.

Jesus was a storyteller, and his capacity for a good story can never be reduced to rational analysis. Jesus felt at home in the world of story, because his own identity was born out of story, namely, the story of creation in all its relational fertility. Only when we choose to liberate Jesus from the tedium of the rational can we truly come to know the Wisdom-sage of divine illumination. Enlightened by that wisdom, life will look different, and then we can begin to let go of the ardent but misguided attachment we have for the world of rational thought.

Fourth Chain

The Captivity of Absolute Dogmas

> It would never have occurred to anyone to doubt God's existence if theologians had not tried so hard to prove it.
>
> —*Anthony Collins*

> Before the total mystery of God, no religious figure and no single religion can call itself the final and full word.
>
> —*Stanley J. Samartha*

CHRISTIANS TEND TO BE JUDGED, and often judge themselves, by their allegiance to creedal faith, already evident in the confession of early Christian times: "Jesus is Lord." Liturgical formulae from the early church focus on the power and rulership of God, transmitted through Jesus, appropriated by the church and imposed upon the faithful. After 325 C.E., the Nicene Creed became a universally approved formula. It became the "closed statement" of Christian belief that has prevailed to our own time.

Faith or Power?

The creed is a constellation of dogmatic truths, deemed to be binding for all time and, consequently, not subject to review or modification. It comprises a set of assertions declaring the supremacy of

God, beginning with the Creator, understood as supreme ruler, and ending with those protecting dogmatic truth now, namely, church authorities. *Power*, not *faith*, is the core value that creeds enunciate and proclaim.

The Christian creed promulgates the male primacy of the Creator, endowed with absolute power. The power is passed on, unadulterated, through the male line of succession, via the only-begotten Son. The Holy Spirit, despite its feminine significance in so many faith traditions, is construed as a dominant power legitimizing the church in its rulership of the people of God. The intention is to empower the people with the gift of faith, but this approach actually *disempowers* people making them passive recipients of doctrinal truths rather than cocreators in an evolving spiritual destiny.

In the patriarchal dogmatic model, growth in faith is determined by verbal assent to creedal statements, by conformity to a set of religious practices and by allegiance to a religious system that can easily breed a culture of codependency. Undoubtedly, Christians have often broken through these restrictions, internalizing their faith through a commitment of heart and mind rather than one based primarily on external observance. Precisely from that same inner journey, comes the first suspicion that the dogmatic model is often misguided and frequently misses the challenge of following Jesus authentically.

This is the exploratory juncture described by many scholars as a "hermeneutic of suspicion." So much of what has been said and written about Jesus looks suspiciously akin to the patriarchal mode of governance. It begins with absolute clarity about the one at the top, the protection and promotion of the ruling power, a clear chain of command from the top down, with a group at the base who live and behave with unquestioning obedience.

Even a cursory glance at the Synoptic Gospels will reveal that Jesus does not belong to this paradigm. Even a cursory awareness of early Christian history will indicate that the Jesus story has been truncated and domesticated to suit the dominant culture. Biblical scholarship for much of the twentieth century began to accommodate the hermeneutic of suspicion and honor its desire for a more transparent quality of truth. For mainline Christian churches this has become a disturbing and often paranoid issue, as they seek to nourish and command the allegiance of the faithful.

Although the sense of suspicion is widespread in the contemporary Christian world, it is not at all clear what the next move is. Once we acknowledge a patriarchal imposition and seek to retrieve the pre-patriarchal Jesus, the whole Christian edifice begins to feel shaky, insecure, and unreliable.

The Jesus story has been so infiltrated with the dominant will-to-power, without the conventional trappings it feels fragile and insubstantial. Worse still the Jesus story, liberated from the patriarchal accretions, comes to be understood as an attack on patriarchy itself. The real Jesus begins to emerge from the imprisonment of oppressive subservience.

Being Christ to Others

Sometimes gradually, sometimes quite suddenly, a different Jesus begins to unfold. An egalitarian revolutionary, endowed with intuitive wisdom, shifting consciousness toward the radical empowerment of the weak and marginalized, thus posing an unprecedented threat to the established forces of power and control. The Kingdom of God looks different now, not a kind of benign dictatorship ruling in the name of right, but the empowerment of the masses that "can bring down the mighty from the their thrones and exalt the *anawim*" (Luke 1:52). The reversal could hardly be more potent!

Dogma carries little weight or relevance for the masses crying out for fresh hope. In their world, preaching Christ or teaching Christ carries no long-term meaning; *being Christ* to them is what will make a difference. And being Christ to the other is not a rational option of the head but an emotional, inspirited response from the heart. At the end of the day it is love rather than "truth" that endures!

Dogmas have helped to hold Christians together in faith communities, but it is not the dogmas that animate and inspire. Living faith belongs to the heart rather than to the head. People grow in faith through encounters with others whose fidelity to Christ is a lived experiential witness rather than fidelity to a set of truths. Christian faith is a lived experience rather than intellectual assent to a creedal formula.

Christians tend to judge each other—and outsiders—by what they "believe in." This immediately sets up a favored in-group and an inferior group of outsiders. This social and religious classification is the basis for so much racism, bigotry, and sectarianism in our world; blood has been shed because of it and wars waged over it; and in its name every religion has resorted to witch-hunts and brutal exterminations. Little semblance here to the radical inclusiveness of the Jesus who commanded us to love even our enemies.

Fortunately in our time growing numbers of people give little attention to dogmas, whether religious, political, or scientific. As people become more educated and critically aware, they are loath to believe something simply because it is an unquestioned truth for the governing institutions of our world. For Christians of our time this is both a liberating and confusing moment. Intuitively, they know that that which they have abandoned had to be abandoned, but what to replace it with is often an agonizing search. Nothing short of a whole new evangelization—an adult catechesis—can meet these people in an empowering way. And the churches and religions are unlikely to respond appropriately until they begin to release both Jesus and themselves from the captivity of absolute dogmas.

FIFTH CHAIN

The Captivity of White Imperialism

Any statement about Jesus today that fails to consider blackness as a decisive factor about his person is a denial of the New Testament message.

—*James Cone*

Only a Christianity that sees itself in the context of the world religions will make sense in the twenty-first century.

—*Chester Gillis*

THE ROMANIZING OF THE CHRISTIAN CHURCH has had a staggering impact on Christian iconography. Everywhere in Africa, where

Christianity has penetrated, churches to this day are adorned with figures of a white male Christ, bearded and robed like the ancient Romans or like medieval European lords. Equally widespread is the caricature of a white European Mary poised in humble subservience. Both Jesus and Mary were people of Palestinian ethnic origin of dark skin and distinctive non-European features.

In Catholic countries such as Brazil and the Philippines, popular fiestas honor Jesus and Mary in processional ceremonies with several features of royal accolade borrowed directly from the cultures of Spain or Portugal. Mary is often heavily dressed and crowned as a queen ruling from on high, a rather cruel irony in cultures where the cult of the Great Mother Goddess flourished in ancient times. This latter belief lies just below the surface of daily experience (as many missionaries will attest) and is quickly evoked through the customs and stories of indigenous people; it is perhaps nowhere more tangible than in the extensive devotion to the Black Madonna, as in the contemporary articulation of Our Lady of Guadalupe in Mexico (see Kennett 2003).

The Task of Retrieval

The whiteness and maleness of Jesus became indisputable facts, although the former was a gross misrepresentation and the latter a gender imposition inflicted by the dominant will-to-power. Biologically, I am not disputing the gender of Jesus; what I wish to challenge and confront is the biological reductionism to which Jesus was subjected. In several ancient spiritual traditions, religious leaders, like shamans and shamanesses were often understood to be bisexual or androgynous. Ancient Indian art and Chinese art are replete with such figures.

This is not an attempt to create a type of patchwork quilt in which Jesus will be all things to all people. It is not a case of trying to reinvent a contemporary Jesus who will be black for the sake of black people or bisexual for the sake of those whose sexual orientation does not fit the prevailing norms. My goal is not reinvention but rediscovery, retrieval rather than modernization. If Jesus is the incarnational representative of the God who cocreates throughout the whole of creation, and laterally throughout the six million years of human evolution, then we need to create a human story of that Jesus that honors those archetypal, primordial realities. There is no place for cultural, less so patriarchal, reductionism in the Jesus of the New Reign of God.

In her desire to reclaim a more foundational understanding of Jesus, the contemporary American artist Janet McKenzie portrays her *Jesus of the People* as a black androgynous person (see *National Catholic Reporter,* Dec. 24, 1999). Not only is this portrayal more congruent with the archetypal identity of Jesus, but it also honors the historical alliance of God in Jesus with our ancient ancestors as we evolved in eastern Africa over several million years.

Our Holy Land of Africa

As God's beloved people, covering a time line of some six million years, most of our story belongs to Africa. The black color of human skin is far more basic to our enduring identity than the Caucasian façade infiltrated through and through with colonization and distortion. The demonizing of blackness often perpetuated by missionaries in bygone days still feeds the culture of racism, while the growing identity crisis of white males in the contemporary world strangely feels like poetic justice. The darkened skin color—whether in its Asian, African, or Latino context—is a powerful enduring symbol of what it means to be human. Our shared solidarity with the darkness of skin is not a token of primitive inferiority; indeed, the very opposite—it is the primary pigmentation that we humans have known for most our time as creatures, blessed, loved, and affirmed by our creative God.

Intellectually and academically, Jesus scholarship, like Christian theology in general, is still very much a preserve of white Western specialists. Even leading scholars of Latino, Asian, and African origin adopt the European Western understandings. Most efforts to comprehend Jesus in the context of the Southern Hemisphere tend to begin with the colonized version of the West. Tragically, what then tends to happen is that the indigenous southern story is a dressed-up version of the European prototype. This is no longer satisfactory.[7] We need to honor the Jesus who archetypally belongs not to the land of Israel, and less so to Western Europe, but to the primordial soil of East Africa, where humans first evolved some six million years ago.

The white European Jesus is a caricature of the patriarchal desire to divide and conquer. We need to disrobe the kingly figure, addicted to the power and glory of triumphalism, and reclaim the vulnerable suffering servant befriending humans on their journey to true freedom. In a culture of multifaith dialogue, we need a Christ who can dialogue with diverse cultures, just as the earthly Jesus had a place at the inclusive table for people of every creed, color, and cultural condition.

SIXTH CHAIN

The Captivity of Male Exclusiveness

> Surely anyone who wants to emphasise Christ's maleness in order to establish prerogatives of males ("priests") over females has not understood Jesus as the liberator of all people, men and women, and has not understood the way he liberated us.
>
> —*Bernard Häring*

> The heart of the problem is not that Jesus was a man but that more men are not like Jesus.
>
> —*Elizabeth A. Johnson*

IN THE PREVIOUS SECTION, I described the maleness of Jesus as an aspect of white Western domination. But, in fact, it involves a great deal more. For some thousands of years before Jesus, males alone were considered to be full human beings. Males alone possessed the "seed" through which new life could be procreated. Women were merely biological receptacles for the fertilization of the male seed—a view endorsed by Aristotle, St. Thomas Aquinas, and Martin Luther. Moreover, children were widely regarded as property—with male offspring being distinctly more valued than females.

For Jesus, therefore, to be Messiah—that is, of God—he had to be seen as descending through a male line. This is described in Matthew's Gospel with the inclusion, amazingly, of three female characters (Rahab, Ruth, and Bathsheba, the wife of David, whom he had seduced from Uriah) whose moral standing is at best ambiguous (see Johnson 2003, 221ff.). Jesus' birth upon earth had to transcend the female reproductive process, which, at the time, was not deemed to be of real importance and from a religious viewpoint was fraught with impure and sinful consequences.

These archaic and destructive beliefs, and their inculturation into the life and ministry of Jesus, tend to be subverted in the romanticizing of the birth and childhood of Jesus. Angelic figures, a "virgin" mother, swaddling clothes, shepherds, wise men, and so on all help to distract us from the radical immersion of the divine in our midst. The provocative indwelling of God in and with the human is either spiritualized toward the heavenly realm or exalted into the royal accolade of the earthly sphere. In both cases the victor is the imperial male culture of the day.

Imposing a Male Stereotype?

The context left the historical Jesus with little choice other than to be cast as a typical male. But the Jesus who proclaims and lives out of the vision of the Kingdom of God is clearly not a male in the conventional sense. He adopts none of the stereotypical male behaviors of dominance, control, rationality, and remoteness (see Plumwood 2002, 72ff.), or even the prerogative of male propagation of the species. Instead, he engages intimately and passionately with people and the culture of the time, especially with those disempowered by the prevailing political and religious regimes.

Instead of guarding power, Jesus gives it away; instead of rational discourse, he tells stories; instead of claiming rabbi-like status, he reaches to the lowliest; instead of excluding the rabble, he includes them—even at table fellowship! Even the tax collectors, sinners, and prostitutes seem at home in his presence. This is not merely a male Jesus with soft edges. This is a Jesus whose very identity is radically different from the norm of human personhood that prevailed at the time. *Relationality* rather than rationality illuminates his entire story.

But there is something more to the identity of Jesus, a dimension that has eluded scholars for most of the Christian era. As an inspirational spiritual figurehead whose impact far exceeds his Jewish indigenous culture, Jesus carries an archetypal significance that transcends time and space. This archetypal identity is frequently observed in the lives of mystics, shamans, and sages. "Intoxicated with God," so to speak, these are people who are nonetheless deeply rooted in earthly reality and leave a lasting impact on human life and culture.

Such people tend to exhibit a sexual identity that frequently escapes the attention of scholars. The stereotypical dualism of male versus female is transcended in favor of an androgynous integration that relativizes both the male and the female in the ideological rootedness of basic biology.

The Androgynous Jesus

The *androgyne* is one of the most misunderstood and maligned concepts in contemporary studies of gender and human sexuality.[8] Ever since the time of Aristotle, human sexuality has been considered to be primarily a biological capacity, with the sole and explicit purpose of human reproduction. While the social sciences tend to adopt a more integrated understanding of human sexuality, the biological emphasis still exerts cultural superiority, making notions like androgyny (and homosexuality) appear deviant and unnatural.

In the androgyne, biological identity is clear-cut. It is the psychic energy that has shifted significantly. The creative inner energy orients the generative capacities beyond the stereotypical roles of male or female. Androgynes exhibit more feminine qualities. They relate more inclusively and tend to organize in a more egalitarian way. They feel very much at home in the spiritual realm, stretch horizons of meaning, and are good at accommodating paradox. They disturb orthodoxies of every type and inevitably are perceived as odd and a nuisance to be kept at a safe distance.

Like several great mystics and sages, Jesus exhibits several features of the androgyne, thus relativizing his uniqueness as a male in the conventional sense. That which constitutes his biological identity as a male is secondary to his psychic generativity as an androgyne. Not only does this relativize his maleness, but, more important, it transcends his maleness—and also femaleness as a purely biological concept—in favor of a more profound way of being human beyond the shrinkage of biological reductionism.

I suggest that it is this androgynous identity of Jesus, more than any other feature that has eluded Christendom for almost two thousand years. Biologically based maleness is one of the most cherished tenets of patriarchy. It has wreaked havoc on the sacred uniqueness of men and women alike. But it has also left us with some grossly misguided notions about leading spiritual figures in all the great religions, few of whom really belong to the cult of patriarchal maleness.

Of all the "chains" I am seeking to loosen in the reflections of these pages, I suspect that of Jesus the androgyne will be the most knotted and tangled of all. Patriarchal cultures seem to feel distinctly uncomfortable when sexuality comes into the discourse. This is taboo material big-time, especially for the religions and churches who thrive on sexual repression.

That very capacity, which is so central and sacred to every human and is the basis of human creativity for time immemorial, is clearly one of God's most cherished gifts. A Jesus devoid of an exuberant, joyful sexuality would strip incarnation of its meaning and integrity. Whatever the price by way of misunderstanding or reprimand, we must not compromise the creative sexuality of Jesus.

SEVENTH CHAIN

The Captivity of the Cult of Redemptive Violence[9]

Religion has claimed to love life while pursuing death—and has kept the rules in place by terror.

—*Robin Morgan*

Can one imagine a more obsessional phantasm than that of a God who demands the torturing of his own Son to death as satisfaction for his anger?

—*Antoine Vergote*

WOMEN SHED BLOOD in order to give life; men tend to shed blood in order to take away life. In several ancient cultures blood is deemed to be the primary channel of the universal life force. In human hands that life force is often abused and misused, and to placate the angry life-giver on high, bloodletting, or blood-shedding, became a widespread ritual of appeasement and propitiation.

Thus, the notion of *sacrifice* became a central feature of ancient and modern cultures. It is widely assumed that the ritual of blood-shedding is as old as humanity itself. This is a sweeping generalization based on little or no evidence, and it exhibits a typically warped analysis extensively endorsed by oppressive cultures. The notion of blood sacrifice as an act of appeasement can be traced back to the shedding of animal blood so that humans could survive.

How ancient this belief is depends on how we date the rise of hunting as a human undertaking. Basing research on extant tribal groups, scholars tend to assume that we humans have always hunted for food and killed animals to procure food. However, evidence suggests that as recently as Paleolithic time (40,000–10,000 B.C.E.) humans gathered food from the resources of plant life and may not have killed animals except when other forms of food were in scarce supply. The myth of the ravaging hunter may be one more hypothetical projection for which there is little real evidence. (See further Ungar and Teaford 2002; Whiten and Widdowson 1992.)

Pacifying the Deity

Ironically, slaying of animals does seem to have been extensively practiced during early agricultural times (from about 8,000 B.C.E. to the present time). Although a great deal more food was acquired from the land, the desire for meat also prevailed. It was during this time that the shedding of blood took on distinctive religious significance. Society was ruled fairly extensively by fiercely aggressive males, whose strategy was validated by belief in a sky God. This God rapidly became like themselves, overpowering, strong, demanding, and cruel.

To court the favor of this demanding ruling deity, strategies of pacifying him came into vogue. Animals were the primary victims, and the firstfruits of the season also were offered. On rare occasions humans were sacrificed, as we see in the Old Testament, with Abraham bringing his son Isaac for sacrifice. Thus the notion of the scapegoat came into vogue, probably around 5,000 B.C.E.

The concept of sacrificial scapegoating has been extensively studied, notably by René Girard (1977; 1986; 2001) and his disciples. Girard traces the notion of scapegoating to mimetic desire, leading to rivalry and violent behavior; the mechanism of scapegoating was required to resolve the threat of destructive violence. For Girard and Christian scholars attracted to his ideas the death of Jesus becomes the ultimate act of sacrifice that renders scapegoating unnecessary and thus redundant forever.

Girard has been criticized on several counts (see Bartlett 2001; Wallace 2002), particularly on the simple observation that the Calvary climax of violence and scapegoating has not diminished the power of violent suffering in the world. Indeed, quite to the contrary, the cross is often hailed as the justification for colonial oppression and the right of the powerful to lord it over the weak.

A much more obvious flaw characterizes Girard's analysis, namely, the fact that he bases all his research on evidence gleaned from the past five to ten thousand years and seems to rely exclusively on scholarship that dismisses as irrelevant anything that happened before that time. However, his attention to the cultural mechanisms of scapegoating and victimization as major problems for our time can scarcely be exaggerated.

An Anthropocentric Projection?

The notion of blood sacrifice is very much an invention of patriarchal times for which there is scant evidence before ten thousand years ago. Prior to that time, the life force was understood in much more generic terms of air, water, and fire—metaphors a great deal more congruent with how modern physics understands the universal life force. Bloodletting and sacrifice began to evolve under an anthropocentric worldview that claimed that "man" is the measure of all things. In the human, blood seems to be the life energy; consequently, it must be the life force of everything else in creation, including the ruling God himself.

The shedding of blood came to be seen as a means of restoring lost balance, setting things right for the offended one. The notion of "victory" crept into the vocabulary, particularly for the ruling vindictive God and his representatives on earth. Thus, we see throughout the Hebrew Scriptures a God who is pleased with the slaying of the enemy and whose glory is enhanced by the victory of the sword. This is a far cry from the Goddess of Paleolithic times, whose bloodletting was unequivocally at the service of prodigious generativity!

In the Jesus story, those two ancient strands become entangled and confused. The metaphor of new life resonates deeply with the radically new vision embraced by Jesus under the rubric of the Kingdom of God. But Christian theology quickly lost sight of that focus on life, as the rhetoric of salvation by death on a cross rapidly gained momentum. From there on, the sacrificial language became widespread as notions like "obedience through suffering," and "sacrificing all for Jesus" became central ingredients of Christian discipleship.

The Option for Nonviolence

For Jesus, however, *nonviolence* is at the heart of this new dispensation, in which we are all called to love and forgive even our enemies. So threatening was the dream to the Roman and Jewish authorities that they eliminated Jesus, hoping that his dream would also come to naught. But the message was more enduring than the messenger, and the early Christian church, preoccupied with a cult of heroism, became enthralled with the violent death of Jesus, largely unable to grasp the dynamic power of a life radically lived to the point of death. They missed the message of the *life* and ended up exalting the *death* as the primary catalyst for redemptive liberation.

For the subsequent two thousand years, the myth of redemptive violence captivated the human imagination. Salvation is perceived as coming through the cross, wrought by the one made perfect through suffering, obedient to an irascible father figure to the point of shedding his last drop of blood. The sordid parody of patriarchal revenge is written all over this widely held belief.

The cult of redemptive violence has inspired many to shed their blood and give their lives for the glory of God and the salvation of humanity. On closer examination, this is very much a male martyrology promoted by a male-led church. Because women often refused to collude with redemptive violence, their desire for a nonviolent outcome tends to be put down to female fickleness. Women's commitment to improving and advancing the quality of life through care for the land, mothering, homemaking, caring for the sick and poor, and educating the marginalized, has rarely been acknowledged as the real work of the gospel. It is not heroic enough to satisfy a bloodthirsty, sacrificial system.

If we diminish the significance of Jesus' death, are we not undermining the very meaning of resurrection? This is another assumption we need to revisit. If we honor, as Jesus did, the primary role of the Kingdom of God, which is about life radically lived to the full, then resurrection is not so much about the vindication of his death as about the affirmation of a life lived in utter fullness. Resurrection belongs to the life rather than to the death of Jesus. In a similar vein, resurrection is an affirmation and celebration of the fullness of life as exemplified by Jesus and offered as a new horizon of creative engagement for all who follow the pathway of Jesus.

EIGHTH CHAIN

The Captivity of Ecclesiastical Domestication

> The model that leads us to look for the grounding of this world somewhere outside it—and seeks assistance from supportive divinities—would appear to be destined for oblivion.
>
> —*Ivone Gebara*

If the church has no message of justice to proclaim to a ruling authority that practices injustice towards its people, the church has opted
out of the politics of God.

—*C. S. Song*

C HRISTIANS TEND TO VIEW JESUS as the founder of a church without which they feel they cannot follow Jesus in an authentic
way. Following Jesus has become concomitant with allegiance to
one or other Christian denomination. All the Christian churches
belong essentially to the culture of early Roman society and, over
time, have become heavily domesticated by the cult of European colonization.

Consequently, Jesus came to be understood as a ruling Lord—the
preeminent king—all-powerful and all-knowing, Constantine's *pantocrator*. As Easterbrook (1998) graphically illustrates, these are all
human projections that distort and camouflage the servant Christ
whose liberation belongs to egalitarian empowerment rather than to
sovereign rulership.

A New Reign of God

Nowhere has the domestication been so corrosive as in its impact on
what the Gospels describe as the "Kingdom of God."[10] This is the
paradoxical subversive strategy that makes Jesus truly unique
among all the faith systems known to humankind. By the time of
Constantine, the project of the Kingdom of God was well and truly
co-opted into the Roman imperial system. To our own day the
Christian faith has been compromised by that cultural and political
accommodation.

The strategy of Jesus was both paradoxical and subversive. It was
paradoxical in the sense that the liberation for which the Jewish people yearned would be delivered not by imperial intervention but by
an empowerment from the ground up; in time such liberation would
subvert the very need for a ruling class. The achievements of the past
would not guarantee its fulfillment; it belongs to a new way of see-

ing that draws hope and inspiration from what Haught (2000, 96–104) describes as the lure of the future.

It was subversive in both a political and a religious sense. Politically, Jesus seems to have adopted the royal imagery of the culture while defying and undermining the royal patronage to its very core. The one and only time Jesus approved of his followers calling him a king (in the Synoptic Gospels), he chose to ride on a donkey whereas kings always rode on a horse. He embraced the cult of kingship but turned it totally on its head.

Religiously, the behavior of Jesus must have astounded and confused the people of his culture. Scripture scholars veer toward the assumption that Jesus relished his Jewish context and cherished his Jewish faith. It seems to me that the evidence for this assumption is at best circumstantial (see Keck 2000, 42ff.) and at worst a projection of the scholars' own need to have faith rooted in a religious tradition.

Throughout the parables and miracle stories Jesus is forever breaking religious rules and flouting religious tradition. He clearly infringes several religious laws of ritual purity and never offers either an explanation or an apology for his reckless behavior. He may have gone to the temple (or synagogue) to pray and worship but often accompanied by outcasts, whose very inclusion became an act of defilement of the holy place.

As a popular preacher, he invited people to allegiance to God not by abandoning their place in the world but by embracing it in the name of love and justice. According to John's Gospel, Jesus was committed to the fullness of life—above and beyond any and all systems.

I am attracted to the notion, which I first encountered in a provocative work of Thomas Sheehan (1986), that in promulgating the vision of the Kingdom of God, not only was Jesus transcending his own Jewish religion, but he was effectively turning his back on all religion. Boff (1980, 98) echoes similar sentiments in the following words:

> Jesus detheologizes religion, making people search for the will of God not only in holy books but principally in daily life; he demythologizes religious language, using the expressions of our common experiences; he deritualizes piety, insisting that one is always before God and not

only when one goes to the temple to pray; he emancipates the message of God from its connection to one religious community and directs it to all people of good will; and, finally, he secularises the means of salvation, making the sacrament of the "other" a determining element for entry into the kingdom of God.

The Vision Domesticated

It seems to me that the twelve in particular never quite grasped what the vision of the Kingdom was about. They wanted Jesus to be a heroic messianic figurehead, and they became increasingly disillusioned when Jesus failed to measure up to their expectations. The basic ecclesiology of St. Paul, encapsulated in small fluid and flexible groups, centered on the Word and on service to the community, in many ways honors the inclusive, liberating vision of Jesus. But already by the beginning of the second century of the Christian era we see the church rapidly becoming institutionalized according to models and paradigms that gradually betrayed the original vision of Jesus. With the incorporation of Christianity into the Roman world in the fourth century, Jesus' vision of the Kingdom had been almost entirely demolished. From there on ecclesiastical domestication took over.

Christendom never completely lost the vision of the Kingdom, and I suspect it never will. Archetypal truth somehow always survives, and despite all the efforts at domestication, it eventually thrives. For much of the high Middle Ages, the fruits of Kingdom seemed to be flourishing in a vast array of mystical, feminist, and justice-oriented movements. The official church of the time was mesmerized by what was going on, and had great difficulty in controlling what was happening. Consequently, church historians—who tend to be males and clerics—describe this period as a dark age of the church. From the perspective of the God's creative Spirit, I suspect it was a glorious epoch of creativity and spiritual growth.

Today, the domestication itself is in disarray. The institutional church struggles to mobilize the credibility of its disenchanted followers. The firm hand of control over the people of God is rapidly losing its grip as people grow up and engage with their faith not as passive children but as questioning adults. Paradoxically, the vision of the Kingdom is flourishing anew after several centuries of sub-version. Adult people are beginning to reclaim an adult faith in an adult God.

The call to adulthood is precisely what the early followers of Jesus found difficult to appropriate. They had been indoctrinated into a type of subservience and "obedience through suffering" that inculcated a type of infantile mind-set. Jesus broke through all that and called his followers to follow suit. But most were unable to rise to the challenge. It has taken up to two thousand years for us as a Christian people to catch up with this adult Jesus leading us forth in a pathway of adult faith. Now, perhaps for the first time in the history of Christendom, we can lay the infantilism to rest. It will not be an easy task, and it is likely to create not one but several ruptures or schisms in the contemporary domesticated churches.

NINTH CHAIN

The Captivity of Middle-class Respectability

> Great pains were taken to mitigate the scandal of God's being revealed in a poor carpenter. His life and sayings were reinterpreted so as to make them more palatable to the rich and powerful. Innumerable legends were built around him, usually seeking to raise him to the level that many understood to be that of the divine—that is, to the level of a superemperor.
>
> —*Justo L. Gonzalez*

> It is the task of Asian Christology to free Jesus for the common people.
>
> —*Byung-Mu Ahn*

THE GOSPELS SUGGEST that Jesus' life ended with a triumphal procession into the city of Jerusalem. It is generally agreed that it was the time of Passover. The city would have been crowded, the atmosphere tense and expectant, and the military on high alert.

Apparently, it was also the occasion when aspiring messianic figures sought attention for their special claim to notoriety. What also seems reasonably clear is that the authorities dealt swiftly and effectively with such messianic contenders. In this case, Jesus would have been promptly arrested—depending on the strength of his subversive claims—and would have been subdued, frequently by death.

When Honoring Is Misguided

The Gospels provide a detailed outline of trials and syndicates purporting charges. Following due process, crucifixion was decreed as the penalty. In the passion narratives of the Gospels, Jesus is being treated as a person of status and social significance. His trials are high-powered events in which maximum justice is being sought for someone very special. This is a Jesus of middle-class status, dignity, and honor.

But was this the real Jesus? And is that how things actually transpired? Is this the radical revolutionary of the New Reign of God? Or is it largely a projection of middle-class respectability, with a story line that became progressively embellished as the oral tradition developed?

As a maverick visionary of the New Reign of God, Jesus shook the very foundations of his inherited culture. I suspect his stories often left people reeling for weeks if not for months. He had a reputation that baffled and confused. Assuredly he attracted large numbers of followers, and yet, as typically happens with prophetic figures, few stood by him to the very end. The message and the messenger became too much to embrace.

As for the authorities in Jerusalem, the religious figureheads certainly had heard of Jesus. Time and again they had tried to eliminate him; now they had a golden opportunity and they seized it. I suspect they did so with little regard for legal or social convention. To them Jesus was a pest, and they would have chosen to get rid of him as expeditiously as possible.

It's Safe to Be Respectable

Two thousand years later Jesus is still held in the captivity of middle-class respectability. Christians are expected to behave according to culturally sanctioned norms of allegiance, fidelity, obedience, and respect. Christians are expected to obey the laws of both church and state, not to question what legitimate authority says, and not to disturb the equilibrium of human systems. Christians are expected to endorse the hierarchical structures that prevail in developed societies and to denounce those who question such paradigms. Christians are expected to be kind and charitable, but too much talk about *rights* and *justice* has a "left-wing" feel to it, and that is perceived as alien to true Christianity.

We have come a long way from the fiery prophetic figure of Nazareth who shocked and disturbed the conventions of his day in the name of justice and liberation. Our respectability has taken a terrible toll on the authentic calling of Christian life. We have lost sight of the deeper vision and lost heart for the passion and enthusiasm of God's New Reign.

The following of Jesus is not a respectable religion, and I suspect it was never meant to be. It is a call to truth, justice, and liberation for those oppressed, excluded, and disempowered. It is primarily for nonpersons seeking acceptance and love amid the brutality and exclusion often invoked in the name of the respectability of patriarchal power.

Christians are called to be different and should be recognized for being different. Once we acquiesce to societal norms and procedures, we have effectively lost our capacity to be salt of the earth and light of the world. We continue the weary, threadbare legacy of domesticating the message of Jesus.

In conventional Christian spirituality, martyr-like suffering is considered to be the unique mark of Christian dedication. While not wishing to underestimate the potential for change that such courageous witness can make possible, the martyr option is based on a spurious rhetoric arising from the theory of redemptive violence. In the present time at least, the option to live for Jesus rather than to die for Jesus is what is truly heroic.

This translates into a radical commitment to the values of the vision of the New Reign of God, seeking to bring about in the world at large the justice, inclusiveness, and equality that seeks a place for everybody, and particularly for the poor and marginalized, at the table of God's abundance. This is the subversive vision for which Jesus gave every ounce of his life to the point of death itself. No greater love can any of us know than that which leaves an indelible mark in carving out a better world for those relegated to the outside.

When we travel down that road, as Jesus did, perhaps the most painful martyrdom will not be in the shedding of our blood, but in the misunderstanding, ridicule, and rejection we will experience at the hands of our very own—family, country, church, loved ones! Christian discipleship is not a popular choice, but for those called, it bears a rightness that sustains the disciple on what can often be a lonely and isolated road.

TENTH CHAIN

The Captivity of Distorted Personalism

> Persons are not isolated but exist only in relation. Hence it is not Jesus's isolated body that is significant but his body interacting with other bodies. The corporate body generated by Jesus interacting with his contemporaries and with us is the incarnation of the Christ-gestalt.
>
> —*Peter C. Hodgson*

> Jesus is brought into being through Christa/Community and participates in the co-creation of it. . . . Hence what is truly Christological, that is truly revealing of divine incarnation and salvific power in human life, must reside in connectedness and not in single individuals.
>
> —*Rita Nakashima Brock*

CHRISTIAN SPIRITUALITY cherishes the notion of a personal relationship with Jesus. It is widely considered to be the mark of a well-developed spiritual life. This well-intended aspiration carries a number of unexamined assumptions, the most basic being the possible projections we make onto Jesus of what we understand personhood to mean—in the context of contemporary Western culture.

The Separated Self

The cherished paradigm of personhood in the West is that of the self-reliant, individualized, rational being, an understanding originally developed in ancient Greece and outlined in the philosophical systems of Plato and Aristotle. This is broadly the understanding of personhood adopted by the church councils (e.g., Nicaea and Chalcedon) in formulating the early christological doctrines. It is the understanding of personhood widely adopted in contemporary Western cultures and in those strongly influenced by Western values. But it is notably absent from the indigenous cultures of Africa, Asia, and Central and South America.

The Greek/Westernized version of human personhood is so much taken for granted, and culturally so validated, that many of us never even dream of questioning its hegemony. Yet there is an alternative understanding that is far more widespread than we assume and far more congruent with our evolving history as a human species. It is often encapsulated in the phrase: "I am at all times the sum of my relationships, and that is what constitutes my identity." This is what I will henceforth refer to as the *relational* understanding; the other approach I will call the *autonomous* understanding.

In the autonomous description, the emphasis is very much on human uniqueness over and against everything else in creation. Not only is this an adversarial orientation; it is also about the human species being superior to all else that exists. The strongest nuance is that of each person being independent and separate from every other and from everything else in creation. *Separation* is probably the single most distinctive feature of the autonomous viewpoint.

Anthropologically, this tends to be based on the view that for much of our evolutionary development we humans were enmeshed in nature, and our coming into maturity required us to be clearly differentiated from everything else. Hence, the notion of *separateness* came to the fore. This is the basis for the severe alienation that humans experience today, especially in the so-called developed nations of the West. By delineating ourselves from nature and setting ourselves over nature, often with the blessing and validation of formal religion, we effectively cut ourselves off from the sustaining womb to which we intimately and integrally belong.

Our concept of autonomous personhood may well be the greatest delusion from which we humans suffer. It is alien to how we have understood ourselves for most of our six million years on this earth. It is largely, if not totally, the product of recent millennia. It is another corollary of the compulsive need to have humans totally in charge. The more we put ourselves in charge the more estranged we become from the cosmic relational matrix to which everything in creation belongs.

The relational understanding of the human strives to honor the relational web of life through which everything is begotten, grows, and thrives. We humans are an integral dimension of that web, but we turn ourselves into threatening pests as we desecrate and exploit so much of the web of life. The painful truth, of course, is that we will not destroy creation, because everything else in creation tends to respect the relational web. It is not creation we will destroy, but *ourselves.*

What Kind of Person Was Jesus?

Christian apologists from the dawn of Christian times assumed that Jesus belonged to the world of autonomous personhood.[11] Hence the desire of the apostles to exalt Jesus on a throne like a kingly figure, something he always resisted according to the Synoptic Gospels. In what must be one of the most persistent strains of ignorance in any religious tradition known to humankind, Christians never seem to have questioned this foundational assumption about the personhood of Jesus. We invoke much rhetoric about being molded in the image and likeness of God, but, in truth, we spend an enormous amount of energy molding God in our image and likeness, and we have done that with Jesus in an outlandish way. In the words of Richard Rohr (2004, 122):

> Jesus came to make a confounding statement about *us,* and we have avoided that message by trying to make profound statements about *him*—statements about which we never all agree and never will agree, but merely argue.

Perhaps one of the most transparent clues in the Gospels in which Jesus hints at a very different self-understanding is the response made to the disciples of John the Baptist in Luke 7:18–22. The disciples put to Jesus directly the question of his identity. Interestingly, he does not answer in what the church has proclaimed to be the great assertion of faith, allegedly spoken by Peter: "You are the Christ the Son of the Living God." Jesus does not give a direct response to the disciples of John the Baptist; he gives a strangely bewildering answer: "Go and see what is happening . . ." (v. 22).

In my opinion, the vital clue is unmistakable. Jesus is suggesting they go and look at his relational matrix, the context in which his life is lived out in liberating relatedness, the engagement with his culture from which Jesus himself obtains his personal, individual identity. Apart from that context, from that relational web, Jesus does not have a personal identity—as suggested in the opening quotations from Brock (1992) and Hodgson (1994).

By extension, we now glimpse a deeper meaning of the notion of the Kingdom of God, the central focus of the life and mission of Jesus. The work of the Kingdom is not something that Jesus is activating in the world of his time. The vision of the Kingdom is an extension of the person of Jesus through which Jesus grows into a unique personal identity. The New Reign of God is Jesus' relational matrix in its largest and most inclusive sense. Hence, Jesus always points the finger away from his individual self toward the Kingdom that is the fullness of his relational self. In the words of Robert W. Funk (1996, 305):

> Jesus pointed to something he called God's domain, something he did not create, something he did not control. I want to discover what Jesus saw, or heard, or sensed that was so enchanting, so mesmerizing, so challenging that it held Jesus in its spell. And I do not want to be misled by what his followers did: instead of looking to see what he saw, his devoted disciples tended to stare at the pointing finger. Jesus himself should not be, must not be, the object of faith. That would be to repeat the idolatry of the first believers.

Jesus belongs totally and unambiguously to the relational way of being human and should never have been imprisoned in the limited construct of the autonomous self. This is the reductionism that in time created a voyeuristic preoccupation with the divinity of Jesus, and it became a gross distraction from the radically new way of being human that Jesus manifested to and for us. This enterprise of engaging with the liberative relational revelation of God in Jesus remains one of the biggest challenges to the Christian faith still awaiting an authentic response from the Christian people.

ELEVENTH CHAIN

The Captivity of Insipid Religiosity

> The feeling of powerlessness is the deepest form of estrangement that our civilisation produces.
>
> —*Dorothee Soelle*

> The world is full of Christians yet nothing changes. It may be time to change the tune. Let's dance with Eve and go in search of Lillith, the first of our foresisters to refuse the embodiment of destructive hierarchy.
>
> —*Lisa Isherwood*

PATRIARCHAL CULTURES tend to breed a climate of codependency. Some are in charge and others are subservient, and to keep the majority in a passive "obedient" role, a rhetoric of parenting predictably arises. We see this in every major religious culture—because all formal religion is heavily influenced by the reign of patriarchy. In Christianity, it is manifest in our designating God as father, the church as mother, our relationship with God as children, and in the adoption of the family as a primary icon for how the faith is to be lived.

In this context, the discipleship of equals has little hope of being honored. The adult as adult will always struggle to find an authentic place. Adulthood is relegated to those who govern, that is, to those who control. And because the control is fundamentally that of a flawed dysfunctional relationship to one degree or another, the rank and file tend to be treated as "children."

A Spirituality of Platitudes

Several behavioral traits now begin to unfold. At this juncture I want to highlight that of insipid religiosity. People tend to be fed with a devotional-type spirituality in which the ruling powers try to assuage all their fears, answer all their questions, and assure them of an eventual divine rescue that will be guaranteed if they remain faithful to the requirements of the ruling group. For most of the time, the people feel unworthy, and that is precisely how the ruling elite wants them to feel. People resort to devotional practices to win the favor of the ruling deity. Their engagement with God and with life is all a matter of preparation for fulfillment in a life to come.

Jesus and the Christian story have been condemned to the same infantile-type spirituality. Jesus is popularly depicted as a gentle, obedient child in a family system that honors the priority of the ruling male, with Jesus himself being declared the firstborn. His fidelity to his indigenous Jewish faith is assumed to be unquestioned, although several factors in the Synoptic Gospels, especially in the parable stories, openly show Jesus criticizing and disregarding some central tenets of his own faith. The church to this day continues to assert that Jesus wanted a new religion in his name, a claim that cuts little ice for serious scholarship and for a growing body of intellectually enlightened Christians.

Spiritual literature tends to adopt John's Gospel with excess fervor, claiming that Jesus was continually in a deep prayerful relationship with the God he addressed and honored as father. Therefore the Christian life is considered to be first and foremost about the spiritual, "personal" relationship with God, making engagement with the social, political, or even interpersonal spheres largely redundant and irrelevant. It is at this level that the vision of the Kingdom of God is most severely compromised. Salvation comes to be seen as something uniquely individualistic, and responsibility for God's creation is dismissed as being a distraction from the real work of salvation.

The culture of insipid religiosity will not easily be dismantled. Respectfully, I acknowledge that this kind of spiritualized hope is what sustains and nourishes millions of people in the poorer parts of the planet. It helps them to retain some semblance of meaning and hope in the face of the horrendous odds of oppression and injustice. The cruel irony is that it offers no solution to their plight. It keeps them resigned to something they should fiercely challenge and oppose—as Jesus would wish them to do. Instead they become lured into thinking that this is God's will for them, and often this is the view endorsed by evangelical preachers proclaiming a convoluted compromised faith that has little to do with the liberating Jesus of the Gospels.

Compassion for Liberation

If we truly honor the Jesus of the Kingdom of God, what we encounter is a spiritual visionary afire with the living Spirit of God, animated with the intense passion of the prophet, enlightened with the deep perception of the mystic, and grounded in the slime and texture of the living earth. Truly this is God with the people, the Emmanuel in a fiercely real way. This is not a God for devotional seclusion, for evangelical rhetoric, or for heady academic analysis. This is a God of engagement, participation, liberation, and compassion.

Compassion is an interesting quality of Jesus. The Greek word *splanchnizomai* is a verb, not a noun as in the English translation. Cultural domestication frequently adopts the strategy of reducing verbs to nouns. It has frightening consequences for the vision of Jesus. Honoring the original Greek verb *splanchnizomai*, "compassion" means an intense visceral empathy with the suffering of the other. Jesus feels the agony of their pain in the depth of his own stomach, an experiential connection that drives one into passionate action to rectify the cause of the suffering. "Compassion" is a word full of guts, vitality, righteous anger, and an insatiable desire to see justice done. It has nothing to do with *pity* or with *mercy*, the insipid words often used to translate this otherwise fiery term.[12]

Of all the urgent needs for the Christian church today, none is more pressing than the need to reclaim the prophetic face of Jesus. Anything less is only another form of perpetuating the cult of insipid spiritualism and the ideology of compromise. It will rock the very credibility of the church as it has existed for the past two thousand years, but Jesus is bigger than that context; and at the end of the day it is the Jesus vision that matters. And whether the church opts for reform or not, the Jesus story, in its bold originality, will continue to be told, to grow, and to flourish.

Twelfth Chain

The Captivity of Black Domination

> The colonizers stripped Africa of its culture, religions and economic systems, but kept patriarchal power intact, if not reinforced, by Christianity.
>
> —*Marcella Althaus-Reid*

> Many African Christologies are so concerned with the past cultures of Africa that they become irrelevant to our contemporary African needs and concerns.
>
> —*John Onaiyekan*

C HRISTIANITY IS RAPIDLY becoming a religion of the Southern Hemisphere. In 1960, 66 percent of Catholics lived in the white Westernized world; today 75 percent live in the Southern Hemisphere, and other Christian denominations follow a similar pattern. Potentially, this presents us with an incredibly exciting spiritual challenge. It requires a fundamental redefining of how we understand our Christian inheritance and how we live it out in the contemporary world.

As we progressively transcend the white ethnicity that millions assume to be endemic to Christian identity, we will encounter some daunting but liberating questions. The new cultural context will expedite the reappropriation of a different understanding of incarnation. Historically, the incarnation of God in our species is a solidarity with blackness more than with any other ethnic identity. God's solidarity with humanity throughout the six million years of human evolution has been predominantly an endorsement of black ethnicity in the Southern Hemisphere.

The Delusion of Power

Yet the black cultures today are precisely the ones that betray Jesus big-time. The black churches perpetuate a devotional religiosity, that is largely at variance with the realities of daily life and very weak on confronting major questions of justice in the world. The growing body of black clergy tends to perpetuate power and control to a degree that makes Western imperialism look tame and benign.

The logic is tragically shortsighted. Adopting the philosophy of inculturation, a concept largely propounded by Western missionaries, African bishops and priests look to their local chiefs as primary models. In African cultures, the chief commands absolute power and unquestioned authority. He is revered and honored as if he were a deity in his own right. African clergy claim that this is a unique aspect of their culture and belongs deeply to their history and traditions.

This is their great delusion. It does not belong to their traditions, and a little history will readily indicate that it doesn't. It belongs to the era of European colonialism, when the colonizers elevated the chiefs from being social and spiritual animators of their communities to being ruthless tyrants who would collect taxes and impose the will of the colonizers in other regards. This is where the big chief got his powerful prerogative—not from Africa itself but from the patriarchal West.

Internalized Oppression

This patriarchal monopoly has infiltrated every domain of human culture, and while Westerners become disenchanted with its hegemony, in several parts of the two-thirds world of Africa, Southeast Asia, and South America, it still allures people with a deadly attraction. This is the lure of *internalized oppression*. Those who were at one time the victims of oppression still carry the pain and trauma of that oppression in the deep subconscious. It has to come out in one form or another, and for those unaware of how internal processes work, one's own kin, one's own people and culture can all too easily become the victims of the subconscious projections.

In our desire to be as good as the oppressors, we subconsciously repeat the strategy of the oppressors. The external structures and systems of the oppressing forces may have been removed. It takes a great deal longer to liberate the shackles that bind us within.[13]

Under the colonizing rule we internalized the need to be subservient and obedient; we were indoctrinated into thinking that this man-made dispensation was actually of God. Unknowingly we can continue to perpetuate this deadly ideology, which has nothing to do with an incarnational God and everything to do with the incarnation of colonialism.

In several cultures of the Southern Hemisphere—Christian and otherwise—there is a cultural expectation that women dress in a manner whereby they expose as little as possible of their bodily endowments. This is another cultural imposition fueled by the patriarchal desire to make and keep women invisible. It is heavily reinforced and protected by mainstream religion. Women themselves defend it fiercely as a way of being respected and respecting one another. This explanation holds little water and serves as a classic example of the kind of rationalization that becomes all too common when internalized oppression is neither named nor acknowledged.[14]

For Christians in the Southern Hemisphere, this is a moment for supreme discernment. Oppression can last for centuries, precisely when it has been normalized and even exonerated as a cultural norm. This can never be justified as the will of Jesus. This is a compromise of the liberating vision of Jesus and of his total abhorrence of the patriarchal value system in all its vestiges.

Demographically, the future of Christendom is in the lands of the South, but whether the Christian South can honor the radically liberating vision of its founder is a formidable question for which current prospects do not look good. However, the Jesus story has an indomitable resilience, and there is every reason to hope that the South, infused with the breakthrough wisdom of the Great Spirit, will take up the prophetic challenge, and that it will do so sooner rather than later.

Notes

1. Several scholars have already been piecing together an alternative Jesus story for our time. These include Bohache (2003), Borg (1994b), Crossan (1991, 1994), Cunningham (1999), Davies (1995), Edwards (1995), Haight (1999), Heyward (1999), Hodgson (1989), Isherwood (1999), Johnson (1992), Powell (1998), Wink (2001), and Witherington

(1994). For a multi-faith perspective, see Haight (1999) and Kuster (2001). Today much of the pioneering work on the historical Jesus is pursued in the United States by the Jesus Seminar Forum (see the Web page http://religion.rutgers.edu/jseminar). Several scripture scholars dislike the factual, businesslike approach of the seminar. Ironically, what sometimes feels like a reductionistic approach to the life and times of Jesus has produced a range of scholarly insights deeply imbued with mystical and prophetic sentiment. See, e.g., Borg 1994a; Crossan 1994; Funk 1996; and the valuable overview of Hoover 2002.

2. Human origins is a hotly debated issue right now. Contemporary paleontologists seem to be broadly agreed that our ancestors of 4.4 million years ago were authentically human (see White, Suwa, and Asfaw 1994). Many regard that as a rather conservative date, averring that it is only a matter of time until we have reliable evidence to stretch the origins further back. A strong clue for the expanded evidence surfaced in July 2001, when the French paleontologist Michel Brunet excavated a human skull in Chad, North Africa. Tentatively it has been dated to be in the range of 7 to 7.5 million years old. For more information, see www.cradleofhumankind.co.za/mw. In the light of this research, I am adopting a tentative date of six million years for the origins of the human species.

3. Christians tend to use the term *incarnation* in a narrow anthropocentric sense to describe the coming of Jesus in human flesh like ours. A number of contemporary scholars concur with Ducan Reid (Edwards 2001, 79–83) that it is biblically and culturally more responsible to apply the concept to all forms of *embodiment*, including the cosmos and home planet, and not just to the human body.

4. Situating the Jesus story in the context of the new cosmology has been attempted by Ruether (1992), Toolan (2001), and Wessels (2003).

5. For more on this topic, see Grosso 1992; also www.ciis.edu/pcc/studentslwebb.html and http://www.angelfire.com/Teilhard.

6. Storytelling is among the most ancient techniques used by humans to communicate and connect. It is a strategy adopted by all the great religious leaders and by sages over several millennia. Today the capacity of story to empower and liberate new meaning is uniquely evidenced among indigenous peoples in several countries. The power of story to awaken and articulate meaning has been explored in recent times by Bruchac (2000) and by Estés (1994). There are several informative Web pages on story and the wisdom of storytelling, e.g., http://web.lemoyne.edu; www.storyarts.org.; and www.creatingthe21stcentury.org.

7. For much of the twentieth century, the patriarchal approach to theology and scripture was the subject of critical analysis, but for the most part pursued by white male scholars themselves, mirroring, while seeking to challenge, the assumptions of the formal Westernized academic world. In recent decades, the horizon has widened to include women and several scholars of various ethnic backgrounds. Only in the last decade of the

twentieth century were nonacademics, rank-and-file members of society, allowed to have a say, one that is still somewhat marginalized in several academic contexts. This countercultural upsurge is sometimes referred to as "*Queering*" or "*Queer theory*" (Web pages: www.queertheory.com; www.queerbychoice.com/qtheorylinks). Its application to the Jesus story has been reviewed by Althaus-Reid (2001; 2003), Bohache (2003), Goss (1994), and Isherwood (1999), among others.

8. Androgyny is popularly perceived to be an extreme form of sexual confusion whereby a person behaves in a manner incongruent with his or her biological identity as male or female. As distinct from a transexual person, who feels trapped in the wrong body, the androgyne's erotic energy is focused not on external embodiment but on an internal psychic intensity, which cannot be culturally accommodated in conventional male/female roles. The deepest aspiration of the androgyne is the total integration of masculine and feminine, male and female. We are into the realm of mysticism. This is not some bizarre human condition characterized by confusion and maladjustment; if anything it is ultra real, but conventional wisdom is unable to come to terms with it. For more on this topic, see Avis 1989, 26ff.; Heilbrun 1993; Singer 2000.

9. Throughout the present work the theme of redemptive violence frequently arises. My main sources are Bartlett 2001; Brock 1992; Girard 1977; 1986; 2001; Schüssler Fiorenza 1994.

10. A great deal has been written on this topic. I find particularly helpful Fuellenbach 1995; Song 1993; and Keck 2000.

11. Surprisingly, very few theologians seem to address this issue. The best appraisal I have come across is that of Hodgson (1989; 1994).

12. Borg (1994b) offers a very creative and dynamic understanding of *compassion* as a quality in the life and ministry of Jesus.

13. More on this topic in Gil 1998; also the Web page www.uvm.edu/culture/site/privilege.html.

14. Womanist theologian Kelly Brown Douglas (1999) provides a useful and informative overview of how internalized oppression undermines black people's understanding of human sexuality, while Jeremy Ayers (2004) examines the wider impact of dualistic thinking on the black body.

References

Althaus-Reid, Marcella. 2001. *Indecent Theology*. London: Routledge.
———. 2003. *The Queer God: Sexuality and Liberation Theology*. London: Routledge.
Avis, Paul. 1989. *Eros and the Sacred*. London: SPCK.
Ayers, Jeremy. 2004. "Towards a Eucharistic Politics of the Black Body." *Theology and Sexuality* 10:99–113.

Bartlett, Anthony W. 2001. *Cross Purposes: The Violent Grammar of Christian Atonement.* Harrisburg, Pa.: Trinity Press International.

Boff, Leonardo. 1980. *Jesus Christ, Liberator: A Critical Christology for Our Time.* Maryknoll, N.Y.: Orbis Books.

Bohache, Thomas. 2003. "Embodiment as Incarnation: An Incipient Queer Christology." *Theology and Sexuality* 10.1:9–29.

Borg, Marcus. 1994a. *Jesus in Contemporary Scholarship.* Valley Forge, Pa.: Trinity Press International.

———. 1994b. *Meeting Jesus again for the First Time.* San Francisco: HarperCollins.

Brock, Rita Nakashima. 1992. *Journeys by Heart: A Christology of Erotic Power.* New York: Crossroad.

Bruchac, Joseph. 2000. *Tell Me a Tale: A Book about Storytelling.* New York: Harcourt.

Clifford, Anne. 2001. *Introducing Feminist Theology.* Maryknoll, N.Y.: Orbis Books.

Crossan, John Dominic. 1991. *The Historical Jesus: The Life of a Mediterranean Jewish Peasant.* San Francisco: Harper.

———. 1994. *Jesus: A Revolutionary Biography.* San Francisco: HarperCollins.

Cunningham, Philip J. 1999. *A Believer's Search for the Jesus of History.* New York: Paulist.

Davies, Stevan L. 1995. *Jesus the Healer: Possession, Trance, and the Origins of Christianity.* London: SCM Press.

Douglas, Kelly Brown. 1999. *Sexuality and the Black Church: A Womanist Perspective.* Maryknoll, N.Y.: Orbis Books.

Easterbrook, Greg. 1998. *Beside Still Waters: Searching for Meaning in an Age of Doubt.* New York: William Morrow.

Edwards, Denis. 1995. *Jesus the Wisdom of God: An Ecological Theology.* Maryknoll, N.Y.: Orbis Books.

———, ed. 2001. *Earth Revealing—Earth Healing.* Collegeville, Minn.: Liturgical Press.

Estés, Clarissa Pinkola. 1994. *The Gift of Story: A Wise Tale about What Is Enough.* New York: Ballantine Books.

Fuellenbach, John. 1995. *The Kingdom of God: The Message of Jesus Today.* Maryknoll, N.Y.: Orbis Books.

Funk, Robert W. 1996. *Honest to Jesus: Jesus for a New Millennium.* San Francisco: HarperSanFrancisco.

Gil, David G. 1998. *Confronting Injustice and Oppression: Concepts and Strategies for Social Workers.* New York: Columbia University Press.

Girard, René. 1977. *Violence and the Sacred.* Baltimore: Johns Hopkins University Press.

———. 1986. *The Scapegoat.* Baltimore: Johns Hopkins University Press.

———. 2001. *I See Satan Fall like Lightning.* Maryknoll, N.Y.: Orbis Books.

Goss, Robert. 1994. *Jesus Acted Up! A Gay and Lesbian Manifesto.* San Francisco: HarperSanFrancisco.

Grosso, Michael. 1992. *Frontiers of the Soul: Exploring Psychic Evolution.* Wheaton, Ill.: Quest Books.

Haight, Roger. 1999. *Jesus: Symbol of God.* Maryknoll, N.Y.: Orbis Books.

Hampson, Daphne, ed. 1996. *Swallowing a Fishbone? Feminist Theologians Debate Christianity.* London: SPCK.

Hart, Kevin. 2001. "The Kingdom and the Trinity." *Australasian Catholic Record* 78:321–39.

Haught, John F. 2000. *God after Darwin: A Theology of Evolution.* Boulder, Colo.: Westview Press.

Heilbrun, Carolyn G. 1993. *Toward a Recognition of Androgyny.* New York: W. W. Norton.

Heyward, Carter. 1999. *Saving Jesus—From Those Who Are Right.* Minneapolis: Fortress Press.

Hodgson, Peter. 1989. *God in History: Shapes of Freedom.* Nashville: Abingdon Press.

———. 1994. *Winds of the Spirit.* London: SCM Press.

Hoover, R. W., ed. 2002. *Profiles of Jesus.* Santa Rosa, Calif.: Polebridge Press.

Isherwood, Lisa. 1999. *Liberating Christ: Exploring the Christologies of Contemporary Liberation Movements.* Cleveland: Pilgrim Press.

Jantzen, Grace M. 1998. *Becoming Divine: Towards a Feminist Philosophy of Religion.* Bloomington: Indiana University Press.

Johnson, Elizabeth A. 1992. *She Who Is: The Mystery of God in Feminist Theological Discourse.* New York: Crossroad.

———. 2003. *Truly Our Sister: A Theology of Mary in the Communion of Saints.* New York: Continuum.

Keck, Leander E. 2000. *Who Is Jesus? History in the Perfect Tense.* Columbia: University of South Carolina Press.

Kennett, Frances. 2003. "Sor Juana and the Guadalupe." *Feminist Theology* 11.3:307–24.

Kuster, Volker. 2001. *The Many Faces of Jesus Christ: Intercultural Christology.* Maryknoll, N.Y.: Orbis Books.

Plumwood, Val. 2002. *Environmental Culture: The Ecological Crisis of Reason.* New York: Routledge.

Powell, Mark Allan. 1998. *Jesus as a Figure in History: How Modern Historians View the Man from Galilee.* Louisville: Westminster John Knox.

Rohr, Richard. 2004. *Soul Brothers: Men in the Bible Speak to Men Today.* Maryknoll, N.Y.: Orbis Books.

Ruether, Rosemary Radford. 1992. *Gaia & God: An Ecofeminist Theology of Earth Healing.* San Francisco: HarperSanFrancisco.

Schüssler Fiorenza, Elisabeth. 1994. *Jesus: Miriam's Child, Sophia's Prophet: Critical Issues in Feminist Christology.* New York: Continuum.

Sheehan, Thomas. 1986. *The First Coming: How the Kingdom of God Became Christianity.* New York: Random House.

Singer, June. 2000. *Androgyny: The Opposites Within.* New York: Nicholas-Hays.

Song, C. S. 1993. *Jesus and the Reign of God.* Minneapolis: Fortress Press.

Swimme, Brian, and Thomas Berry. 1992. *The Universe Story: From the Primordial Flaring Forth to the Ecosoic Era—A Celebration of the Unfolding of the Cosmos.* San Francisco: Harper.

Toolan, David. 2001. *At Home in the Cosmos.* Maryknoll, N.Y.: Orbis Books.

Ungar, Peter S., and Mark F. Teaford, eds. 2002. *Human Diet: Its Origin and Evolution.* Westport, Conn.: Greenwood Press.

Wallace, Mark I. 2002. *Fragments of the Spirit: Nature, Violence, and the Renewal of Creation.* Harrisburg, Pa.: Trinity Press International.

Wessels, Cletus. 2003. *Jesus in the New Universe Story.* Maryknoll, N.Y.: Orbis Books.

White, Tim D., G. Suwa, and B. Asfaw. 1994. "Australopithecus Ramidus: A New Species of Early Hominid from Aramis, Ethiopia." *Nature* 371:306–12.

Whiten, A., and E. M. Widdowson, eds. 1992. *Foraging Strategies and Natural Diet of Monkeys, Apes and Humans.* Oxford: Clarendon Press.

Wink, Walter. 2001. *The Human Being: Jesus and the Enigma of the Son of Man.* Minneapolis: Augsburg Fortress.

Witherington, Ben, III. 1994. *Jesus the Sage: The Pilgrimage of Wisdom.* Minneapolis: Fortress Press.

2

Jesus and the Quantum Worldview

We enjoy a growing awareness of our identity in relation to the cosmic whole to which we belong.

—*Ivone Gebara*

In quantum reality, relationship is truly creative. It is here in the realm of relationship, that quantum reality is most mind-boggling and revolutionary.

—*Danah Zohar*

I N CHAPTER 1, I PLAYED the role of a deconstructionist, seeking to remove the ideologies that get in our way as we seek to follow Jesus in the twenty-first century. It has taken us some two thousand years to catch up with Jesus, which in evolutionary terms is quite a good achievement. Now that we are at this evolutionary threshold of Christian faith and the search for meaning that it evokes, we face a fresh moment of reconstruction. This is a formidable task, which I will strive to honor on two levels: (1) to reclaim the archetypal context of the original Jesus—that is the subject of the present chapter;[1] and (2) to allow the Jesus story to be retold for the context of the twenty-first century, which will constitute the third and final section of this book.

The vision and strategy of the Kingdom of God (hence: the Kingdom) seem to be the most authentic way to access the deeper meaning of Jesus both for his time and for ours. This is the vision out of which everything else unfolds. This is the reality of Jesus writ large, so large in fact that it has taken humans two thousand years to begin to reclaim its awesome and practical implications. Jesus touches the core of our human destiny, but does so in a cosmic and planetary context; and these are the dimensions I wish to explore in the present chapter.

Jesus and the Quantum Physicist

Quantum physics provides a fertile landscape for this undertaking. It liberates us—and Jesus—from the arid, congested mind-set of patriarchal rationalism. It sets free the creative Spirit to dream and imagine, to intuit and discern. It liberates the story, so that all the specific stories that Jesus left radically open can now be told afresh. In the previous paradigm we were condemned to following the mechanistic principle which claims that the whole equals the sum of the parts. Now we are at the service of a new consciousness in which the whole is greater than the sum of the parts.

Quantum physics emerged out of a growing disillusionment with the narrow horizons of classical science. The theory is widely recognized among scientists and has been verified by several experiments. It also forms the basis of some of the most innovative technologies that influence our lives today, including computerization, global information connections, and laser medicine, to mention but a few. Despite these very real and highly successful applications, most scientists still pursue a strategy whereby quantum theory can be subjected to the classical worldview. It is so difficult to accept and live with something as elusive and creative as the quantum vision.[2] Even the full philosophical and mystical implications of this vision have rarely been acknowledged, much less affirmed. In adopting the quantum vision, we embrace a different way of relating with our world and its meaning for us:

a. The neat, fixed, unchanging face of reality yields pride of place to fluid flows and quantum fluctuations of creative energy, driven by forces that we humans, at this stage of our evolution, do not even understand, much less control.

b. We transcend the world of rational deductive reasoning—cause and effect don't work any more as we thought they did, and still think they should.

c. We encounter a world where every whole is greater than the sum of its parts, and individual parts make little or no sense in their lonely isolation.

d. We are called to befriend a relationally oriented creation in which the capacity to relate is an indelible feature.

e. We engage with the particle-wave duality as cocreative participators, always modifying what we engage with, to a greater or lesser degree.

f. We inhabit a cosmos of nonlocality (Nadeau and Kafatos 1999), in which effects happen at speeds greater than the speed of light and according to dynamics in which the flapping of a butterfly's wing at one end of planet earth can effect the course of a tornado at the other end.

g. We encounter a wisdom greater than our own, a consciousness that belongs primarily to cosmic creation and laterally to the human brain (further explored in O'Murchu 2002, 169–81).

Deepak Chopra (2000, 39), provides a neat and succinct summary of the quantum vision:

> Creation manifests
> Energy exists.
> Time begins
> Space expands from its source.
> Events are uncertain.
> Waves and particles alternate with one another.
> Only probabilities can be measured.
> Cause and effect are fluid.
> Birth and death occur at the speed of light.
> Information is embedded in energy.

In this new vision there is no power over, only power with. Playing the power games of patriarchal domination is deeply alien to the nature of life as exemplified in the quantum vision. Our insatiable desire for control makes no sense in a universe where everything exercises its own sense of control precisely because everything is out of our control. We live in a self-organizing universe where we humans need to have the humility and wisdom to submit our plans to the greater wisdom of the cosmic and planetary systems (see Kauffman 1995).

Jesus in the Quantum Context

When we release Jesus from the chains of two thousand years of Christendom what might he begin to look like? Perhaps, St. Paul in the second letter to the Corinthians can pave the way for our reflections:

> From now onwards, therefore, we do not judge anyone by the standards of the flesh. Even if we did once know Christ in the flesh, that is not how we know him now. And for anyone who is in Christ, there is a new creation; the old creation is gone, and now the new one is here. (2 Cor. 5:16–17)

Already in his own lifetime, it seems that Paul was inviting people to regard Jesus differently from the prevailing norms of both personhood and creation. Individual personhood in the flesh was no longer adequate, but neither was the "old creation." Christ's coming on earth had altered the prevailing terms of reference. The new creation, what the Gospels call the Kingdom of God, augured changes so original and provocative that it has taken Christians—and humans in general—some two thousand years to catch up with them. Now we must reclaim the new horizon and learn to live by it!

The Gospels suggest that the following are some of the contextual elements that need to embroider a critical and credible Jesus story for our time:

1. Relatedness

All the great religions grapple with the relationality of the divine, but none of them seems to get it right. The desire for power and control always gets in the way. The relationality of the divine is best gleaned, I suggest, by scrutinizing the capacity to relate that imbues the whole of creation. We detect this on the microcosmic scale in the quarks and leptons: they thrive through interrelating, not through Darwinian-type competition. We detect it again on the macro scale. George Greenstein (1988) points out that configurations of three adorn the galactic and planetary spheres. Little wonder that humans began to envisage Trinity as an archetypal statement through which we discern the divine life force as fundamentally relational in nature.

I suspect that the understanding of God as a power-for-relationship is the oldest understanding of the divine known to human beings—predating formal religion by thousands, if not millions, of years. It is from that primitive, archetypal awareness that doctrines and dogmas of the Trinity eventually evolved.

Christian history and theology reduced our understanding of the Trinity into a type of mathematical quagmire, in which the separation and individuality of the three "persons" became more significant than their relatedness. Jesus tends to be located close to the Father God, unambiguously asserting domination rather than his interconnected relationship. We then end up with a relegation of the Creative Spirit as subservient to Jesus, despite the fact that the New Testament never declares that to be the case.

The Jesus for our time needs to be embedded once more in the trinitarian relational matrix. Jesus belongs to the realm in which the whole is greater than the sum of the parts and should never have been expunged from it. Similarly, Jesus belongs to the whole of creation, which itself is the first and oldest creative expression of the divine creativity. How precisely the relatedness of Jesus differs from that of Father and Spirit may well be one of the most meaningless questions ever asked. The need for clear difference is a human patriarchal need, which I suspect is a major barrier to our primary God-given task of learning to befriend our relational God, striving to birth a more wholesome relationality throughout the length and breadth of creation.

2. Birthing

Relationality describes something of the fundamental being of God and of God in Jesus. How do we describe the activity of God? Again, creation's story suggests that birthing is a primary activity of the divine and one of the more dynamic metaphors to describe the divine at work in creation. Meister Eckhart captivated the notion beautifully when he posed the question "What does God do all day long?" to which he answered: "God lies on a maternity bed giving birth all day long" (quoted in Fox 2000, 41).

Again, creation is our great teacher here. In the birthing forth of God over several "billennia" we see a universe of prodigious and elegant creativity. And it is not without its paradoxes, reminding us that paradox, particularly that of the creation-destruction couplet, is written into the tapestry of creation at every level (see O'Murchu 2002, 94–109). Yet the will-to-life, the potential for birthing always triumphs, and there is every reason to believe that it always will.

This divine capacity for birthing new possibility led the peoples of Palaeolithic times to envisage God primarily as an erotic woman exuberant in her fertile energy. She came to be known as the great Earth Mother Goddess. Remnants of her once glorious reign still endure in human culture, especially among indigenous peoples (see Christ 1997). Despite the relentless efforts of patriarchal religion to demonize and eliminate her, she holds her place in the spiritual consciousness of the human soul and is likely to make a triumphant comeback in the opening decades of the twenty-first century.

The rediscovery of the great Goddess will be marked by a renewed appreciation and understanding of the sacredness of the earth itself and its ingenious capacity to survive and thrive despite all the manipulative destruction of the human species. Already theologians are connecting with the wise energy that infuses creation, religiously articulated in the wisdom traditions of several of the great religions and, for some, uniquely embodied in the Jesus of Christianity (e.g., Edwards 1995; Johnson 1992; Schüssler Fiorenza 1994).

This is not a gender issue about whether the divine is male or female. This is about the human capacity and need to image God. Because we ourselves are also of a divine creation our images are likely to reflect something of the divine reality, assuming of course that we honor the divine at work in creation. Imagery around the maleness of God, with fatherhood as a primary attribution, and the divine tending to be reserved to the anthropocentric world is unlikely to be of God; it is largely, if not totally, based on projections of the dominant patriarchal culture of recent millennia.

God's birthing forth, therefore, is more readily accessed through females than through males, while acknowledging that both genders contribute to the creative process of organic life. Birthing is very much a motherly energy—hence the image in several religious traditions of the woman fiercely protecting life whether in the soil or in the human. To this same end, Grace Jantzen (1998) reminds us that "redemption" comes not through *mortality*, with the emphasis on death and suffering but through *natality*, celebrating the birthing, flourishing, and growth of everything in creation.

3. Incarnational Time

Because the primary activity of the divine is that of birthing forth, then the universe is saturated with life and endowed with abundance. It is there at the microscopic, quantum level, largely invisible to the human eye and almost totally inaccessible to scientific scrutiny. It becomes manifest through various channels of energy and movement and ultimately manifests in embodied forms of which the cosmos itself is the primary body and in turn cocreates with the divine to bring forth a vast range of other creatures, including human beings.

Consequently, the notion of embodiment does not apply just to humans. Creation is replete with a vast range of embodied expressions, dating backing several billion years. Insofar as embodiment is a primary requisite for incarnation, then God has been incarnating within creation for several billion years. We need to rescue the notion of incarnation from the appalling minimalism to which we have condemned it.

We use the concept with a narrow, exclusively anthropocentric meaning, reserving it not just for humans, but for the select few that have populated planet Earth over the past two thousand years. But our God has been birthing forth life for time immemorial, and the divine solidarity with the human species dates back at least six million years. So, why all the reductionism? Why the blatant idolatry? Why not honor God's time scale rather than the crude reductionism of recent millennia?

For Jesus, I suggest that time is archetypal rather than linear. Perhaps this is why the scriptures distinguish between *kairos* (sacred time) and *chronos* (linear, quantifiable time). In a sense Jesus belongs to the time-less realm; from within that context, assuredly, he can identify with our circumscribed sense of time, but as the Jesus story unambiguously attests, Jesus is forever inviting us to transcend those narrow, stultifying boundaries. Unfortunately, Christendom identified these "time-less" horizons with "the world beyond" thus imposing their dysfunctional cosmology on the worldview of Jesus, which was significantly more elegant and embracing.

The rational human mind considers real only that which it can measure and quantify. The divine mind obviously works on different scale variations. Humans tend to stick rigidly to that which is observable and quantifiable. To one end of that spectrum is the microscopic sphere where the four-dimensional space-time continuum breaks down at those thresholds where we humans suspect that there are other time dimensions, but at this stage of our intelligence we are unable to decipher them. One tentative naming are the six to seven curled-up dimensions proposed by string theorists (see Green 2000). On the large macro scale, the four-dimensional space-time spectrum proves to be a good deal more useful, but now with the discovery of nonlocality, in which we know that things happen faster than the speed of light, this model is also proving to be inadequate.

I am not trying to argue that the missing time dimensions, which intuition tells us are there, can be used as proof for the existence of a divine mind. Arguments based on the need for rational proof belong to the patriarchal mind-set. That type of wisdom belongs to the past. The wisdom that engages us now, for which Jesus serves as an exemplary model, is something much more akin to the vision out of which quantum theory was born. It is the wisdom of the big picture that honors diversity, paradox, open-endedness, and mystery. This is the space in which our relationship with the divine, Christian and otherwise, stands the best hope of growing in wisdom and maturity.

4. Discipleship (the Kingdom)

The previous three notions—relatedness, birthing, and incarnation—weave into an original synthesis in the largely misunderstood rubric that was the primary focus in the life and ministry of Jesus. The Gospels refer to it as the Kingdom of God. Contemporary scholars, particularly women, find the language and imagery of royalty distasteful and reminiscent of oppression and patriarchal domination. Since Jesus clearly sought to transcend such manipulative power, it is puzzling that he should have stuck so closely to these condescending notions.

Jesus may have deliberately adopted and used the royal terminology as a strategy of subversiveness. All the Christian churches have sanitized Jesus, domesticating him in what could broadly be described as a well-behaved adult of middle-class culture. Respectability toward convention, order, and authority feature strongly in that culture. This leaves no room for the Jesus of the parables, who stretched all the conventional norms, broke many of the respected religious rules, and shocked people into a radical inclusiveness of partnership and reconciliation.

This was the disturbing, prophetic Jesus. This was the Jesus who set out to make all things new, thus at times demolishing quite mercilessly the norms and institutions that got in his way. Could it be that as Jesus flew in the face of all the royal, kingly standards, he reappropriated their language and imagery, but now turned upside-down so that they were effectively not recognizable anymore? By retaining the kingly jargon, Jesus parodies the very dispensation he seeks to demolish. This is a poetic device frequently used in prophetic contestation (see further Funk 2002).

The "kingly" realm now belonged to a different power, not power over, but power with. John Dominic Crossan describes the Kingdom of God as a companionship of empowerment, in which people were liberated and empowered to birth forth new creative possibilities for that same creation in which the divine life force had been birthing since the dawn of time. No ruling classes anymore, no select favorites for the royal enclosures, no preferential treatment for those who came at the first hour. Equality reigns supreme, in the name of a love that gives unconditionally and invites all to the greatest challenge any of us could ever confront: to love unconditionally as we ourselves have been loved and liberated.

Discipleship now looks very different. It is no longer modeled on allegiance to some noble figure at the top. It is no longer a case of following humbly from behind. Mission in partnership is born, and it is not just collaboration among people but with everything and everybody in the New Reign of God's creation. Love is a key quality, but so is justice, because love without justice becomes sentimental and patronizing. Christian culture likes charity and is quick to admire and acknowledge the charitable person.

In parts of the planet we have been giving charity, with great generosity, for several decades, yet the poor remain poor and impoverished. Why? Because they know not the justice that would ensure that they too should have their rightful share. This is what makes the Kingdom of God so radically different: it is a strategy for practical change, not for pious platitudes. It is a vision for radical transformation, not a panacea for some utopia that keeps people forever hoping in vain.

There is an enormous sense of ambiguity about this vision of Jesus. Did Jesus himself fully grasp what it was all about? Probably not in all the details, and it looks as if he did not get the timing right. The Gospels suggest that he expected it to happen in his lifetime or shortly thereafter, but he was mistaken. What he did get right, however, is that his life and mission marked a profound cultural transformation, with planetary and global implications. The future would be different, while allowing that the radically new future can be realized only by those who adopt the discipleship of Jesus.

Scholars acknowledge this ambiguity in the portrayal of the Kingdom in the Christian Gospels, and I agree with those who see this as a positive rather than a negative feature. It honors the foundational humanity of Jesus, so essential to incarnational rootedness, and entrusts Christians with weighty responsibilities for the future development and evolution of the Jesus vision. Jesus provides a model, a deeply inspiring and challenging one, but one that remains radically incomplete apart from the Christa-community (Brock 1992) that constitutes the Jesus story at each moment in history, including the present one. The Jesus story is not closed; it remains radically open to the ongoing engagement and creativity of each new Christian generation. Among scripture scholars, Leander Keck (2000, esp. 88ff., 110ff.) provides a skillful treatment of these intricate issues.

Human Uniqueness

In the quantum worldview, everything takes its identity from the context of its relationships and not from its self-referential separation or aloneness. As indicated frequently in chapter 1, even Jesus takes his identity from the context of his mission. In the Synoptic Gospels he never points the finger at himself, but always away from himself toward the Kingdom of God. The Kingdom is the earthly name for the relational matrix from which Jesus takes his individual identity.

And with this adventure a whole new definition of what it means to be human comes to the fore. Gone forever is the lonely, isolated competitive individual, an identity that males adopt more readily because of cultural conditioning over at least five thousand years, but an appropriation many women find unfulfilling even to this day. As a species, none of us can embrace fully this identity, because it is not what we knew for most of the six million years we have been on this earth. For most of that time we were an egalitarian species, generically connected with the earth itself and much more benign and cooperative in our relation to all sentient beings.[3]

There is a relational matrix out of which everything in creation is begotten, one important feature being the *convergence* elegantly described by Simon Conway Morris (2003). Theologically we call it the Trinity, not just the Christian "three persons in one" but an archetypal primordial capacity to cocreate, to birth forth, to empower. Humans are born out of this matrix because the earth that brings us forth is itself born from it. The originating matrix is the source of all living reality, including that of the earthly Jesus. The difference between Jesus and ourselves is that Jesus was probably more consciously aware of this relational identity, whereas humans today, indoctrinated with patriarchal stratification, are largely unaware of their true identity.

It is through our capacity to relate that we become what our God wishes us to become. From a Christian point of view, Jesus serves as an archetypal model leading the way and inspiring us in our endeavors. Just as we ourselves have succumbed to the dissection of patriarchal manipulation, Jesus too has been its victim. The Christian churches have molded Jesus and his story into a caricature that would validate and justify their separatist philosophy. The conversion to a more relational mode of living is unlikely to be pioneered by major institutions—religious, political, or otherwise. That new orientation is likely to come from the ground up, from the ground swell of people gradually becoming disenchanted with the fragmenting culture of individualism. Despite the odds weighted against it, this breakthrough may happen much more quickly than any of us alive today can imagine.

Saved by Story

In the history of the human race, storytelling is one of the oldest and most enduring methods of pedagogy (see chapter 1, n. 5). Even before we developed articulate speech we told stories, using the pre-verbal skills of hand and eye, gesture and symbol. And we told stories for a whole range of reasons, but basic to all was an innate search for meaning and purpose. Storytelling more than anything else knits together the fragmented aspects of existence and molds our reality into a comprehensive whole.

Stories are archetypal experiences in which strands of meaning coalesce. The speaker and the hearer are the collaborative agents for a process that liberates meaning. Stories function in a manner somewhat similar to a strange attractor in science, those computer simulations developed by modern scientists to illustrate how the experiences of life pull us toward focused meaning.[4] Stories generate their own driving force, for which the storyteller becomes the creative agent, interdependently drawn forth by the creativity of the story hearer.

At every stage of our human existence the vital energy of the cosmos and the earthly dynamics of planet Earth weave the inner fabric of our being. Story releases what is unfolding in that complex landscape, adding coherence to the evolutionary search for meaning. The story will honor the larger picture and will enable us to discover, time and again, how our individual lives blend in with the relational matrix of cosmic and planetary reality.

Is there a place for God, or the divine, in this process? All the great religions couch their deep truths in stories passed on from messiahs and prophets, from sages and mystics, for example, the parables of the Christian Gospels. Yet, when it comes to major religious institutions like churches, allegiance is assessed not in terms of storytelling, or story listening, but in terms of laws, rules, procedures, and observances. God is often portrayed as an anthropocentric overlord, ruling by rational process as the rulers of this world do.

The religions have passed on sets of formalized stories we call scriptures. They are meant to illuminate the divine and its impact on our lives. But in several contemporary situations, these formalized narratives hide the spiritual appeal of the divine rather than reveal its true nature. What is often illuminated is the projected images of the leading religionists themselves, trying to cow people into submission, robbing people of the creative imagination and paralyzing people in a passivity that undermines both the capacity for speaking and hearing liberating stories.

An example comes to mind from the Christian scriptures (Acts 16:25ff.): Paul and Silas are imprisoned and, like all the other inmates, seem to be tied with chains. In the dark of night the whole building is rocked as if by an earthquake, the prison gate flings open and the prisoners' chains become detached from their moorings. The prison governor panics and is about to commit suicide, when Paul restrains him, reassuring him that all the prisoners have not escaped. In fact they are all quite content just to be in the midst of their new-found freedom.

From that juncture on (16:29), we never again here about the prisoners. All we hear about is Paul himself and his successful ordeals. Meanwhile, the richness and liberating grace of a wonderful story become totally subverted, and the potential for gospel freedom is seriously undermined and eroded. The writer is so enthralled with exonerating the hero (Paul), that he loses sight of the gospel promise of liberation for the oppressed and imprisoned. A unique moment for hope-filled evangelism is virtually obliterated. Tragically, this is what patriarchal culture tends to do to the liberating praxis, the retrieval of which is a major preoccupation for the times in which we now live.

In contemporary Westernized culture, the dynamic of storytelling tends to be subverted. The powers that rule and govern our world cannot tolerate the open-ended nature of stories. They cannot include those who want to participate in the unfolding story, which gets translated into empty rhetorical categories called politics, economics, the hard sciences, and the social sciences. Everything gets reduced to a set of syllogisms, what Mark Jordan (2000) calls "a rhetoric of tedium," serving a petrified, numbed culture where imagination and creativity are at an all-time low.

The Jesus story, too, needs to be liberated from the imprisonment of the petrified imagination. We need to articulate afresh who Christ might be for us today. Not the Christ who is the same yesterday, today, and forever but the one who befriends us as a Christian people grounded in the earth and at home in the cosmos. We need to salvage Christ from the forces of reductionism—religious, cultural, political—that have been extensively used over the past two thousand years of Christendom.

Postmodernism

The reductionism continues unabated, with a new guise for each new time. Currently, one of its more alluring constructs is that of *postmodernism*, lauded by some as a new liberating movement and condemned by others for its fickleness and superficiality. Postmodernism claims that we have outgrown the age of the metanarrative, overarching governing stories that guide our way and inspire our lives. Such narratives are viewed as imperialistic, requiring everyone to follow a broadly similar set of views and behaviors, alien to the pluralism and diversity required for contemporary life. On the other hand, critics of postmodernism bemoan the clear-cut, centralized values, fearing that we are increasingly the victims of cultural fragmentation and meaningless relativism.

I wish to suggest that the postmodernist view is quite a distorted one that is not nearly as widespread as Westerners often assume. Both its proponents and its adversaries seem equally deluded. A few crucial elements need to be noted:

1. All the leading advocates of postmodernism are white, Western males, many of whom have spent their entire lives in sturdy academic institutions away from the real issues of daily life. Females rarely feature, and there is very little cross-cultural research.

2. The metanarrative perceived to be under threat is none other than the Western imperial worldview, which promoted colonialism in the nineteenth and twentieth centuries and today is the driving force behind the belligerent marketeering and advertising of globalization.

3. It seems to me that this movement belongs originally to the upsurge of patriarchal domination some eight thousand years ago, ruthlessly committed to the philosophy of "divide and conquer."

4. Mainstream religion adopted the same basic strategy, with each religion claiming to be the only valid metanarrative, not merely for its own cultural context (e.g., Hinduism for the Indian subcontinent) but for all humanity.

5. Intellectually, Greek culture became the ruling norm about three thousand years ago, prizing the rational, logical, deductive method over the mythological approach, which cherishes imagination and intuition. Rationalism and deductive proof characterize the patriarchal mind-set and the dominant culture down to our own time.

6. The attack by the opponents of postmodernism is fueled in large measure by a nostalgia for the unquestioned right to power that characterized all dominant institutions up to a few decades ago.

7. Positively understood, the multiplicity of ideas advocated by the postmodernist view exercise a purifying effect on all dogmas that have acquired an ideological status; this includes many of the major religions that flourish today. (More on this topic in Gallagher 1997, 88–91).

Contrary to the contention of postmodernists, it seems to me that several metanarratives thrive in our time. These include the new cosmology; the scientific view of quantum theory, a vast collation of data on alternative technologies, e.g., solar power; the Jungian collective unconscious, highlighting the power of universal consciousness; the philosophy of networking; alternative approaches to health-care; multifaith dialogue. Alongside these emerging metanarratives, we need a Jesus story that is congruent with the archetypal yearnings if our time; that I will attempt in the final section of this book.

These contemporary metanarratives pose a threat to the prevailing culture—mainly for two reasons: (1) they offer understandings that are perceived to be so new that they leave little room for the old in any shape or form; (2) they incorporate levels of diversity and pluralism considered to be at variance with an authentic metanarrative. Generally speaking, dominant institutions will ensure that funding for research does not go into these enterprises, because then an alternative truth would be made transparent and that could spell ruination for the dominant powers.

What would a Jesus story look like in the context of these unfolding cultural narratives? All of them aim, to one degree or another, to rectify the dysfunctional relationships that humans have created vis-à-vis the web of cosmic and planetary life. All the movements listed above have the desire for right relationships at their core. This, too, is the central truth of the Kingdom that Jesus set out to establish, the New Reign of God at the heart of creation to which Christ-followers of every age are asked to commit their energy and creativity.

Finally: The Word Becomes Quantum!

This book offers a new metanarrative on the life and ministry of Jesus. What makes it unique, and different from several other metanarratives, is the way it names and re-visions the issue of power. I set the story within the broad frame of the quantum worldview. One of the most revolutionary and baffling features of quantum theory is what its proponents call *the collapse of the wave function*. Broadly, it goes like this. The quantum visionary works primarily with a world of unlimited possibilities and believes that reality—at any level—can be honored only when all possibilities are entertained. Instead of monolithic power it seeks to honor the creative diversity through which empowerment flourishes.

When we opt for one or other outcome, or select one possibility from a range of others, we have collapsed the wave function. According to classical science, we have entered the world of reality—the domain of monolithic truth; according to quantum theory we have abandoned the world of reality, which thrives on creative diversity. In other words, in the quantum realm, the really real is where all things are possible; the unreal world is when we have to choose one or other option because as human creatures we are limited in our resourcefulness, and that is the best we can do in any one situation.

Every time therefore, we collapse the wave function—confer reality on one or other aspect of our experience—we need to remember that it is only a partial realization of a greater wisdom, perhaps one of inexhaustible wealth. What we should never do, therefore, is canonize or immortalize any one aspect of our experience, any one theory, dogma, or set of scriptures. Every time we do that, we alienate ourselves from our cosmic and planetary source; we disempower ourselves in a most destructive way. Tragically, that is what the classical worldview is always encouraging us to do!

The collapse of the wave function is a metaphor for our human predicament, a type of double-edged sword of serrating pain and piercing truthfulness. We can access truth but only in a very limited way—at least at this stage of our human evolution. The greater truth is always out of reach and will be revealed depending on our skill to evoke it. Probably only the mystics can evoke it on the type of larger scale that, mistakenly, the classical theorists think is impossible.

When, therefore, we engage with a particular aspect of formal religion, for example, the life of Jesus, the Buddha, or Krishna, we have collapsed the wave function. We are dealing with one particular rendition, limited by the cultural context of a particular time and place. If we dogmatize it, we are automatically catapulted into the world of idolatry. A quantum rendition of the story has to be different; and whenever, and however, must strive to honor the world of all possibilities. This, too, applies to sacred stories as Richard Rohr (2004, 107) reminds us when he writes: "Sacred stories can always, and must always, be read on many levels to elicit their full transforming power."

Jesus was a creature of quantum embrace. Having broken down the congested boundaries of his day, he left us with a legacy of unfinished business. We are the privileged ones who have inherited that legacy. Just as the great work of creation continues, so does the work of the New Reign that Jesus inaugurated. How do we embrace that challenge in our time? How do we salvage the tradition from the monopoly of patriarchal control? How do we retrieve the enduring truths from the rigidity of dogmatism? How do we reclaim the Jesus whose story we should never have closed in canonized scriptures or in denominational religion?

Perhaps one way to reclaim what has been lost and subverted is to invoke the creative imagination, precisely what Jesus did in his life and ministry. Let the Jesus story be told afresh. Let it be told by an imaginary Jesus of *our time*. Let's not fret about honoring the tradition because all that is best in what we have inherited is already there in the living tradition. In a sense, the scriptures reveal Jesus in the collapse of the wave function—a particular, historical, cultural rendition. On the other hand, the living tradition embodies the Jesus who is the catalyst for new possibilities.

The Jesus who proclaims and embodies the fullness of life, transcends all the structural contexts of history, whether literary or institutional. Jesus lives primarily in the organicity of creation itself, not just in the human heart but in all the pulsations of creation's heartbeat. It is that enlarged understanding of Jesus that seeks expression in the final section of this book, a narrative that, we hope, honors the Christ of yesterday, today, and every day—in the open-ended future of God's creation.

Notes

1. Etymologically, *archetypal* denotes the most basic and the most original. A concept borrowed from anthropology and Jungian psychology, it suggests that the consciousness of creation is infused with patterns of psychic energy that influence every aspect of life including human behavior. The concept of the creative vacuum in modern physics has a very similar significance (see Laszlo 2004; Swimme 1996, 91ff.).

2. The nonscientific reader will find several contemporary texts exploring quantum theory in an accessible way. I also recommend Web pages www.sfu.ca/chemical/quantum and www.directory.google.com/science/quantum. My concern in the present work, and in my book *Quantum Theology* (O'Murchu 1997, 2004) is about the *vision* underpinning the theory rather than the theory itself. Other writers in this vein include Capra (1976), Zohar (1991); Zohar and Marshall (1994); Laszlo (1993; 1998; 2004), Smolin (1997), and Roszak (1999).

3. Lynn Margulis (1998) claims that the capacity for cooperation and egalitarian behavior can be traced back almost four billion years to the behavior of the original bacteria—hence her concept of *symbiogenesis*. On a similar vein, see the groundbreaking work of paleobiologist Simon Conway Morris (2003), and the evolutionist John Stewart (2000).

4. The concept of the *strange attractor* is a symbolic construct from the interface of particle physics and computer simulation. For a brief description, see O'Murchu (2000) and Wheatley (1992); for a more detailed account, see Butz et al. (1997).

References

Brock, Rita Nakashima. 1992. *Journeys by Heart: A Christology of Erotic Power.* New York: Crossroad.

Butz, Michael R., Linda L. Chamberlain, and William G. McCown. 1997. *Strange Attractors: Chaos, Complexity and the Art of Family Therapy.* New York: John Wiley & Sons.

Capra, Fritjof. 1976. *The Tao of Physics: An Exploration of the Parallels between Modern Physics and Eastern Mysticism.* London: Fontana/Flamingo.

Chopra, Deepak. 2000. *How to Know God.* New York: Harmony Books.

Christ, Carol. 1997. *The Rebirth of the Goddess: Finding Meaning in Feminist Spirituality.* New York/London: Routledge.

Conway Morris, Simon. 2003. *Life's Solution: Inevitable Humans in a Lonely Universe.* New York/Cambridge: Cambridge University Press.

Edwards, Denis. 1995. *Jesus the Wisdom of God: An Ecological Theology.* Maryknoll, N.Y.: Orbis Books.

Fox, Matthew. 2000. *One River, Many Wells: Wisdom Springing from Global Faiths.* New York: Jeremy Tarcher/Putnam.

Funk, Robert W. 2002. *A Credible Jesus: Fragments of a Vision.* Santa Rosa, Calif.: Polebridge Press.

Gallagher, Michael Paul. 1997. *Clashing Symbols: An Introduction to Faith and Culture.* London: Darton, Longman & Todd.

Green, Brian. 2000. *The Elegant Universe: Superstrings, Hidden Dimensions, and the Quest for the Ultimate Theory.* London/New York: Random House.

Greenstein, George. 1988. *The Symbiotic Universe: Life and Mind in the Cosmos.* New York: William Morrow.

Jantzen, Grace M. 1998. *Becoming Divine: Towards a Feminist Philosophy of Religion.* Bloomington: Indiana University Press.

Johnson, Elizabeth A. 1992. *She Who Is: The Mystery of God in Feminist Theological Discourse.* New York: Crossroad.

Jordan, Mark. 2000. *The Silence of Sodom: Homosexuality in Modern Catholicism.* Chicago: University of Chicago Press.

Kauffman, Stuart A. 1995. *At Home in the Universe: The Search for Laws of Self-Organization and Complexity.* New York: Oxford University Press.

Keck, Leander E. 2000. *Who Is Jesus? History in the Perfect Tense.* Columbia: University of South Carolina Press.

Laszlo, Ervin. 1993. *The Creative Cosmos: A Unified Science of Matter, Life and Mind.* Edinburgh: Floris Books.

———. 1998. *The Whispering Pond: A Personal Guide to the Emerging Vision of Science.* Rockport, Mass.: Element Books.

————. 2004. *Science and the Akashic Field: An Integral Theory of Everything*. Rochester, Vt.: Inner Traditions International.

Margulis, Lynn. 1998. *The Symbiotic Planet: A New Look at Evolution*. New York: Basic Books.

Nadeau, Robert, and Menas Kafatos. 1999. *The Non-Local Universe: The New Physics and Matters of the Mind*. New York: Oxford University Press.

O'Murchu, Diarmuid. 1997, updated 2004. *Quantum Theology*. New York: Crossroad.

————. 2000. *Religion in Exile: A Spiritual Homecoming*. New York: Crossroad; Dublin: Gill & Macmillan.

————. 2002. *Evolutionary Faith: Rediscovering God in Our Great Story*. Maryknoll, N.Y.: Orbis Books; Manila: Claretian Publications.

Rohr, Richard. 2004. *Soul Brothers: Men in the Bible Speak to Men Today*. Maryknoll, N.Y.: Orbis Books.

Roszak, Theodore. 1999. *The Gendered Atom: Reflections on the Sexual Psychology of Science*. Berkeley, Calif.: Conari Press.

Schüssler Fiorenza, Elisabeth. 1994. *Jesus: Miriam's Child, Sophia's Prophet: Critical Issues in Feminist Christology*. New York: Continuum.

Smolin, Lee. 1997. *The Life of the Cosmos*. New York: Oxford University Press.

Stewart, John. 2000. *Evolution's Arrow: The Direction of Evolution and the Future of Humanity*. Canberra: Chapman Press.

Swimme, Brian. 1996. *The Hidden Heart of the Cosmos: Humanity and the New Story*. Maryknoll, N.Y.: Orbis Books.

Wheatley, Margaret J. 1992. *Leadership and the New Science: Discovering Order in a Chaotic World*. San Francisco: Berrett-Koehler.

Zohar, Danah. 1991. *The Quantum Self: Human Nature and Consciousness Defined by the New Physics*. London: Bloomsbury.

Zohar, Danah, and Ian Marshall. 1994. *The Quantum Society: Mind, Physics and a New Social Vision*. London: HarperCollins.

3

The Story

When the disciple is ready the guru disappears.

—Gregory Bogart

This demanding God does not know the answers but is alive in the questions.

—Lisa Isherwood

My Relational Matrix

WELCOME TO MY STORY! In the story we are about to explore, I am the narrator and you are a participant in the narrative experience. We are both involved in this story; we each contribute to both its possibility and its unfolding. Yet that story is greater than either you or me. So let's be ready for some stretching of body, mind, and spirit!

Although I am the narrator, we are dealing with a story that breaks open its meaning to a degree that can never be contained in any one narrative. The narrative is more important than the narrator; the story we are about to explore belongs to an epic that has been unfolding for billions of years before the possibility of human composition was even envisaged.

Many human stories are construed around a beginning, a central plot, and an ending. Not so in the case of my story. My reality cannot be confined to those limited human parameters. There is a human version to my story known to Christians for the past two thousand years; every time I talk about it, I will refer to it as my *earthly indwelling*. I find it very limited and it saddens me to watch the anthropocentric ideologies that humans have imposed on that particular manifestation of my presence on Earth.

The Context

To begin with, there is a context to my story, and I would dearly love it if people would make a better effort to honor it. That context is born out of my relational matrix. That is the starting point for everything in life, myself included. So let me begin by telling you about my *relational matrix*.

Relational wholeness is the source of my being, the basis of my sustenance and the very reason for my existence. I belong to a web of relationships, the synergy that energizes every aspect of being and becoming. My core identity—and indeed, yours too—is born out of this ancient all-pervasive relationality. Many of the religions describe it as *Trinity*. This is a human effort—and a rather inadequate one—at exploring what my relational matrix is all about.

Long before your scholars began exploring the idea, you all lived out of this matrix and did pretty well in engaging relationally with it. Intuitively and experientially, you know what this deep relationality is all about. It is imprinted in the very fabric of creation on the cosmic and planetary levels. And since for most of your time, you have lived symbiotically, in a close relationship with the earth, instinctively you know what I am onto.

The problem today is that you pitch yourselves over against creation, and to the degree that you do that you also alienate yourselves from the relational matrix. Tragically, religion is one of the big culprits here. For some thousands of years now, you humans are into this bizarre game of "divide and conquer." You have even tried to divide and conquer my relational matrix. When your Christian theologians adopted this crude mathematical arrangement, trying to fit three into one, I watched with a bemused sense of horror.

You can't reduce my relational matrix into three dominant

strands or manifestations. It is particularly abhorrent to reduce it to three human-like figures that Christians call Father, Son, and Holy Spirit. Three might be a sacred number carrying theological significance; it actually holds a far richer significance in cosmological and scientific terms.

My relational matrix serves as a hub for all relational birthing, the begetting and becoming that have characterized existence throughout the ages of infinity. In this context there is neither beginning nor end. Humans seem to need these parameters, but the creative energy of my relational matrix outstretches all the boundaries known to humankind today.

The Human Role

I have a great deal more to say about the relational matrix, and don't worry, I'll come back to it. The next thing I want to say a brief word about is what Christians call "incarnation." Yes, indeed, I do have a special connection with you, humans, but that special connection did not begin about two thousand years ago, with my earthly indwelling as the Christian Jesus. Oh no, I have been around far longer than that! Sorry to disappoint those among you for whom the Christian Jesus is all-important, but I can't let you get away with a crude reductionism of that type!

In conjunction with my relational matrix, I have been around much longer than your minds can comprehend. I have watched with keen interest your coming to being over several millennia, and I was there in total solidarity when you first evolved as a human species about six million years ago. By the way, please don't try to pin me down to exact times and places, because I don't work according to chronological time. Have you got that one: I DON'T WORK ACCORDING TO CHRONOLOGICAL TIME! Accordingly, I am not much concerned about the precise moment in time when humans first evolved. I understand that the paleontologists date it around six million years ago. Okay, I'll work with that.

Now, humans, can you help me work out this dilemma? Since I was fully there endorsing, affirming, and blessing your emergence six million years ago, why do you restrict my incarnational creativity to the past two thousand years? Worse still, Christians support the idea that my incarnation is confined solely to the one you call Jesus the Nazarene. Why should my relational matrix, prolific in abundance, fertility, and liberating potentiality be confined to one outstanding personality? To me, at least, that smacks more of the triumphalism of the human hero rather than the prodigious creativity of my relational matrix.

So, in terms of incarnation—my total solidarity with your human becoming—I was with you without reserve or regret right from the very start. While you were still climbing trees in East Africa, I was totally with you and that was fun at times—long before religion made life so damn serious! From my point of view, there was never any question of waiting six million years for redemption and salvation to take place. As far as I am concerned, the grace of redemption was yours—FULLY—from the very beginning.

The problem seems to have been that you lost sight of your purpose—your *relational* focus—and you began playing destructive power games, with me, with yourselves, and with the wonderful creation with which my relational matrix has gifted you.

The other thing that puzzles me is this: Why did you betray your African origins? Why have you chosen to be so destructive of your African homestead? And why have you invented so much racism against your black sisters and brothers? You know, you were all black to begin with, and so was I. I love black people and every aspect of their diverse culture. It pains me deeply what you have done, and continue to do, to the homeland of Africa.

So, I hope I am making myself clear. I want to break out of this stranglehold in which you have imprisoned me these past two thousand years. Every time I hear that figure, I feel like screaming. It does my head in! It makes me feel so small and fabricated! I belong to a relational matrix of billions of years and of cosmic expansiveness. My incarnational identity belongs to that context, and not to the reductionistic bottleneck into which you humans have squeezed me. I have come to set you free; please allow me to be free also!

I'll come back to this topic again. It is so crucial. There are so many misunderstandings afloat, and the picture is so narrow and destructive!

My Divinity?

For some of you, I guess I am meandering on and not getting to the point. What you want to know about is my secret power, what your scholars call my divinity. Why are you so curious about that aspect? I sometimes get the impression that your religionists would love to have complete control over my divinity. To be honest with you, I don't have control over it myself, so how could you have? And anyhow, what's all this control about?

I think my divinity is at its best when it's out of control, when the creative Spirit of my relational matrix can blow where it wills. Then exciting things begin to happen. Then relationships begin to flourish, sometimes chaotically, but always creatively.

May I suggest that you stop worrying about my divinity. Both I and the relational matrix will manage that one fine. As I shall indicate later, it is my humanity you should be concerned about. That is the dimension you have not taken seriously. Had you taken it seriously, then in fact you would have no reason to be so preoccupied with my divinity. That is where you humans have got so many things out of kilter.

And Revelation?

Now, another thing that baffles and confuses me, is what your theologians have to say about *revelation*. Actually, I find their arrogance quite disturbing. They seem to be so sure about things I was never too sure about myself. Why this compulsive need to get everything crystal clear?

Things can't be clear-cut in an evolving universe, empowered by quantum fluctuations. Creative freedom requires everything to be open, fluid, creative, growing; and this means that things will be chaotic and confusing at times. I have never had any problem with this, and neither does my relational matrix, so why have you, humans, become so scared and spiritually petrified about your evolving understanding of life?

As for revelation, there never has been a time when the relational matrix was not disclosing a fullness of meaning, but it was always commensurate with the consciousness of the time. The natural world receives that revelation in accordance with the creativity and freedom needed at each evolutionary stage. The enduring feature of every stage is the growth in depth and complexity of the web of interactive and interdependent relationships. My relational matrix forever impregnates creation with a more refined and mature capacity to relate.

Right now, you humans are quite off course in your appropriation of this relationality, and getting it right could prove costly for your species at this stage in its evolutionary development. Of course, you do have a choice on what direction to move things to your own advantage. Right now, however, you just don't have the relational wisdom to make the right choices.

The Reign of Love-Justice

And that saddens me, because in the revelatory maturation associated with the Christian faith, I offered a very clear blueprint for the right relating. The Christian Gospels refer to it as the "Kingdom of God." The Kingdom of God is another rubric through which you can understand my relational matrix, and sadly that's the connection that Christian religionists have missed for most of the past two thousand years.

During the phase of my earthly indwelling, I tried to clarify afresh what the relational matrix is about. A number of women disciples got the message, but it eluded many of the male followers completely. And your historians have all but eliminated the evidence for those wise intuitive women, without whom you would not have inherited a Christian story at all.

The version passed on by the menfolk is largely a projection of their own insatiable desire for dominance and control. They interpreted the notion of the Kingdom of God as a spiritual-ecclesiastical mode of declaring and asserting the power of God through the power of sacred institutions. After Constantine in the fourth century, that deviation reached preposterous proportions. From there on it was "man's" kingdom that mattered, not God's. I don't understand why you humans are so addicted to power.

For me, the Kingdom of God is an inculturation of my relational matrix, offered as an affirmation and confirmation of everything you humans had achieved over the six million years of incarnational and planetary growth. Its focus is about a radically new way of being human, realized of course in your interdependent relationship with planet Earth and the cosmos to which we all belong.

The Kingdom of God is not some kind of project I was trying to activate in the world—outside and beyond my own self. No, the Kingdom of God is me in my relationships with all of creation. It is the sum total of relationships in a whole that is greater than the sum of its parts—and is, therefore, greater and bigger than my "individualized" self. It was not I who brought the Kingdom of God; The Kingdom of God brought me!

I set forth a broad pattern for this new way of relating and I left it radically open for your innovation, imagination, and fulfillment. I tried to explain it through those wonderful stories your scholars call parables. And I never closed those stories. I left them all wide open —waiting for you to bring them to completion. Each parable is like a book of ten chapters; in the Gospels, you have chapter 1; the other nine chapters will be written as you continue to cocreate with my relational matrix and in this way contribute to the building up of the Kingdom in the midst of creation.

It's a shame really that Christians got that one so badly wrong. You see, I never intended the Kingdom for Christians only. I offered it as a pure gift to everybody—as with every gift that comes from my relational matrix. And perhaps, not surprisingly, the people that really went for it were the poor, the marginalized, the disenfranchised, the outcasts. After all, they had nothing to lose, had they? So they went for it big-time! They risked everything, and deep in their hearts they knew it was worth it.

When I said to those creative risk-takers: "Let's sit at table, share our stories, and break bread for each other," well, for a start, they didn't think I'd go that far, and even they were shocked at my cavalier attitude to Jewish table fellowship. They had all this baggage about not being worthy, and feeling unclean, and a list of other prohibitions that would make one's heart groan with anguish.

You mean to say . . .

JOSHUA: Forget all that nonsense about ritual purity and table exclusiveness.

ESTHER: But our teachers have been telling us all these years that if we don't respect our laws we will never inherit eternal life.

JOSHUA: Esther, the New Reign I am inaugurating is not about laws but about values, especially the value of unconditional love.

JACOB: But we need to observe the laws to be able to relate rightly with Adonai. Otherwise we could find ourselves banished forever.

JOSHUA: In my relational matrix there is no place for exclusiveness; there are no favorites and no conditions for entry other than the willingness to love everybody unconditionally, irrespective of creed, race, or color.

ESTHER: But that is contrary to our religion and the tradition of our fathers.

JOSHUA: Esther, I am bigger than religion, and so are you. Today we are all called to worship in spirit and in truth as together we work at recreating our world anew.

I'll tell you something, trying to get that message across was so bloody exhausting, I used to have to escape to the mountains for days in order to recover from the ordeal. Let's be quite clear about this: religionists can erect all the barriers they like and draw up laws until their jawbones get frozen, but for me and my relational matrix, nobody, and no aspect of creation, is excluded. Kings and kingships of this world are welcome to their hierarchies, respectabilities, and fine distinctions, but in my Kingdom all of them are declared bankrupt and redundant. Mine is not a Kingdom of this world; mine is a new way of being that includes the whole of creation. Nothing less would honor the breadth and depth of my relational matrix.

I thought I had made all that clear on that final journey into Jerusalem when I decided to call the disciple's bluff. All this furor about my being a king, and enthroning me on a pedestal as if there were not enough dictators on thrones already! Well, I taught them a lesson when I rode on that donkey—I'll tell you about that one later. After that they should be in no doubt what kingship meant for me.

Okay, I can see a few nodding heads. I guess we have enough to keep us going for the moment! Does anybody have a question?

You mean to say . . .

JUDITH: Sir, you have told us nothing about your mother. I am a feminist and I'd like to know something about your mother.

JOSHUA: Thank you, Judy, for asking. Motherhood is that primordial aspect of my relational matrix through which we forever give birth—to protons, supernovas, bacteria, and bluebells. In my earthly incarnation, Earth is my mother and yours too. And that aspect of the earth-womb that individualized me was my biological mother called Miriam.

JUDITH: And what was her ethnic background?

JOSHUA: In today's terms, she was a Palestinian.

JUDITH: So, she wasn't a white woman?

JOSHUA: Not at all, she was dark-skinned, representing the dark creativity of the earth and the black skin of Africa from which we all evolved. I think I know what you're getting at: the white European Mary, where did she come from? Forget about her, Judy, she is just a figment of the imagination of white Western imperialists—hence the reason why she always looks so holy and subdued!

RACHEL: Are you trying to tell us that earthly origins are of no significance for you?

JOSHUA: Everything that comes from the earth is of enormous significance for me. Biological origins are important, too, but they need to be seen in the larger context of creation.

RACHEL: And what about national identity?

JOSHUA: I don't believe in it. We all belong to the one earth, born of the same stardust; we all share the same flesh, blood, and bone. We all share a similar need to laugh, work, play, and make love. All these divisions are man-made and superficial. We need to get rid of them all.

RACHEL: But we have always been told that the Israelites are
God's chosen people and that ours is the promised land.
JOSHUA: Rachel, why do you believe everything you have been
told? You're an adult. Check it out, and be suspicious of
anything that smacks of human or divine imperialism. For
my relational matrix, there are no sacred lands or chosen
people. All are special and cherished in our eyes.
RACHEL: Well, thank goodness for that!

Yes, there are so many misunderstandings and so many spurious
ideas. For now, please hold on to this idea of the relational matrix.
If we can keep that as the primary focus, then we'll get everything
more or less right in the end. So, allow me to restate the main points
I have made thus far:

1. First, there is my relational matrix; that's the source and sustenance of my being and becoming. It is not so much about my coming forth from the Father; that is a very narrow anthropocentric
explanation. And it has the kind of parental overtones that breed
codependency and prevent people from becoming adult. I don't like
it all.

Let's hold to the relational matrix: the wellspring of all possibility including mine, evidenced foundationally in the creative vacuum
from which the universe itself came forth. My precise role within the
relational matrix is something that has never worried me too much.
I just rejoice in the fact that the synchronistic energy of the matrix
mobilizes every dimension—divine and human —for the benefit of
the prodigious unfolding of everything in creation. The titles "Son,
Savior, Redeemer, and Messiah" all feel reductionistic to me.

Anyhow, there is no place for titles in the relational matrix. We're
not into that kind of thing!

2. Now, from an earthly point of view, the best way to come to
terms with my relational matrix is to go big-time for my vision of
the Kingdom of God. During my earthly indwelling, I lived for the
Kingdom, and I died for it. It was the most ingenious brain wave I
ever had. It has taken my earthly followers almost two thousand

years to come to terms with it, and to be frank with you, that process is only beginning.

3. Only when you get the idea of the Kingdom right can you hope to grasp my sense of incarnational empowerment. You begin to see the depth and inclusiveness of my vision. Of course, my incarnational gifting is not confined to humans. Every form of embodiment —insect, plant, animal, person, planet, cosmos—is a manifestation and expression of incarnational generativity. Without bodies, Spirit cannot flourish. So my relational matrix ensures that embodiment features in everything we have created.

So, that's who I am—in broad outline! And you need to get the big picture right before getting into the details—of my nation, my genealogy, my mother, and so on. This meticulous nit-picking that seems to fascinate you humans, strikes me as being a waste of time and a waste of good energy. Go for the big picture, embrace the mystery and learn to relate with everything that is yearning for authentic relationship; in that way, you won't go far wrong, and we'll all have a happier planet on which to live. Of course if you do go off the rail a bit, don't worry; I won't hold that against you, so don't hold it against yourself!

Shalom, my friends; let's join the Filipino people for a Mirienda!

Poetic Echoes . . .

Long before the scientists broke creation into parts,
Dividing up the universe with subatomic cracks.
Long before cosmologists could grasp the basic facts,
Relationships were rife in the abyss.

Long before religionists got dogma on the run
With doctrines of the Trinity, enrolling three in one.
Long before the theories of who begot the Son,
Relationships were rife in the abyss.

Long before we separated one thing from the next,
Ensuring that the hierarchy would remain forever fixed.
Long before we atomized what previously was mixed,
Relationships were rife in the abyss.

Long before the churches prescribed us to commune,
Alleging that divinity connected through a loom.
Long before the discourse of communion was abloom,
Relationships were rife in the abyss.

For long we've missed the crucial point that relating is the clue
And it's only in connecting that we'll see the whole thing through.
Too long have we ignored the web that always weaves the new,
The Weaver at the heart of the abyss.

EPISODE TWO

My Identity and Yours!

L ET ME TALK TO YOU about identity—my identity and yours, too! That's an issue that causes a great deal of confusion. The basic problem is that you humans seem unable to honor your own origins, which are also my origins. The relational matrix to which we all belong is the wellspring of all possibility, an infinite reservoir of vitality and generativity. That energy flows like the rhythms and movements of a dance. Creation dances into existence as waves of energy begin to weave the complex tapestry of Gods and creatures, stars and galaxies, elephants and bumblebees.

Now the secret to identity is this: everything is interrelated, inter-connected, and interdependent. Nothing makes sense in isolation and never did. There is no such thing as identity in isolation; there is only relational becoming, and in that process life evokes from deep within us the capacities and potentials to endow creation with elegance and beauty. We are made for beauty—everything is designed beautifully, provided, of course, that we honor our rela-tionality, the source from which all beauty emanates.

You mean to say . . .

JAMES: Excuse me, Sir, are you trying to tell me that I don't have any individual identity, that I am not a person in my own right.

JOSHUA: Who you are as an individual and a person arises from the context of your relationships.

JAMES: How do you figure that out?

JOSHUA: Think of it in simple terms; we all needed our parents to enter the world; biologically none of us would exist without the relationship of our parents. But of course we are a great deal more than biology. Our existence is also dependent on the carbon of the stars and the organic energies we have received from so many aspects of cosmic and planetary life.

JAMES: Forget the bloody planets; we're talking about human beings

JOSHUA: But, James, without the stars none of us would be here, and none of us could survive without the energy of the sun, transmitted through photosynthesis, nourishing us in every moment of our existence. Everything is interconnected and so are we.

JAMES: I wish you would keep things simple; I hate it when things get complicated.

JOSHUA: What I'm talking about, James, is complexity, not complicatedness. I am talking about the richness of the relational matrix to which you, I, and everything belongs.

JAMES: To be honest with you, I think I would prefer not to belong.

JOSHUA: We don't have a choice, James, this is the way things are, so take the risk and trust the relating, my good friend!

The capacity to relate is the gateway to meaning at every level. It is written into the fabric of creation since time immemorial. Explosively, exuberantly, and often chaotically, stars and galaxies joined in this relational fiesta many billions of years ago. Planets evolved on their circuitry routes, dancing forth patterns of elegance and intricacy. Organic life, over a time span of almost four billion years, wove a symbiogenetic web with cooperative endeavor written all over it; those ancient bacteria were incredible team workers and, of course, continue to be, mysteriously weaving webs that give pattern and meaning to every living organism.

Humans, you are far too preoccupied with the survival of the fittest. For a start you are not meant to be about survival: it's in giving away your life that you actually reclaim it. Everything in creation evolves, mutates, grows, dies, and is transformed anew in the process of birth-death-rebirth. Everywhere in creation the cycle of birth-death-rebirth undulates amid the troughs and heights of creative achievement. There is no ultimate annihilation, only paradoxical transformation, as we are embraced by more complex waves of interrelating.

What Is a Person?

Just think for a moment about your own becoming. Billions of years ago, stars exploded, radiating into the universe a vast array of dust particles, containing several gases, and one in particular with the innocent sounding name of *carbon*. At the cosmic level, that's where your story—the story of each one of us—begins; the stars are our sisters and brothers. Many billions of years later, the sun and moon enhance the power of cosmic creativity. The carbon gets entwined, relationally, in the photosynthetic miracle whereby nourishment becomes another of life's sustaining potentials.

And let's not forget the moon. Gee, my relational matrix had some fun getting that one right. All those cyclic, elusive energies, relating to tides and oceans, water and vapor, and the menstrual cycles of every woman who has walked planet Earth—all elegantly represented in the moon. What an achievement!

Now with all those foundational elements in place, the lure of erotic love (which, by the way, I never called lust), drew together the people you call your parents. Already in the twinkle of their eyes, their passionate playfulness and the full expression of their sexual pleasure, your individual relational matrix was taking shape. Long before the procreation of your etheric body—the template for your physical makeup—there existed all those dreams, yearnings, longings, and desires: loving, painful, erotic, creative. And then in destiny's own time, when creation was ready to welcome another gift of creativity from our relational matrix, your conception took place.

Your parents were the biological channels through which that complex relational energy was transmitted into a new creature. Essential though the biology is, it is merely the external face of a profoundly complex process, reactivated every time a rose blooms forth, a seedling dies, a turtledove takes the risk of leaving its nest, or the human egg-cum-sperm embeds in the endometrium of the woman's womb.

From beginning to end, each of you is the sum of your relationships and that's what constitutes your unique identity. It took a complex interactive process of several cosmic and planetary energies to bring you into being with your parents acting as the primary channeling agents. And who you become at every stage of your existence is dependent on the quality of your relatedness, not just in terms of other people, but with all the other organisms (including the earth-planet), which impinge upon your life.

You mean to say . . .

AUGUSTINE: But, Sir, you forgot about the soul; where does that fit into your plan?

JOSHUA: I am fascinated by the language you use, Gussy; in a relational universe, things don't "fit in." We are not dealing with some kind of mechanical process, biochemical or otherwise. We are dealing with creative energy that always flows in interweaving patterns. The soul is an energy flow. It holds together the diverse movements of the creative possibilities, guiding them toward optimal realization.

AUGUSTINE: But I always believed, and conscientiously taught, that the soul is a unique creation of God. Am I right or am I wrong?

JOSHUA: A bit of both! Soulfulness is a quality of my relational matrix, but it also becomes a feature of every soulful interconnection that helps to deepen the meaning of relationship.

AUGUSTINE: You have me confused and I hate being confused.

JOSHUA: Gussy, confusion can at times be a very healthy state of soul. It keeps us from being arrogant and dogmatic. It keeps us open and transparent to deeper meaning.

AUGUSTINE: But if everything is that open, how do we know who is actually in charge?

JOSHUA: Creation is in charge and always has been. What more do we need?

AUGUSTINE: I'll tell you something, Sir, if you keep on like this,
   I'll end up not even knowing who I am.
JOSHUA: And Gussy, what a liberating moment that would be.

Soulfulness

Sounds like we need to stay with this identity question for a while,
because I am sure Augustine is not the only one with these kinds of
questions. All this talk about soul versus body or body versus spirit
—I find these dualisms quite repulsive. They break down and break
up that which is meant be a unity, an undivided whole. There is no
distinction between body, soul, and spirit and there never has been.
Everything in creation is impregnated with spirit power, the living
Spirit of my relational matrix. Therefore, bodies don't need to have
souls inserted at some stage in order to make them alive. That's one
of the most crazy notions I have ever come across.

The essential aliveness of things, including human beings, belongs
to the relational energy that weaves in and out of all organisms. Its
source is my relational matrix and its destiny is as universal and
enduring as creation itself. I don't even like that word *soul*; it has too
much guilt-stuff attached to it. Let's talk about soulfulness, that
sense of the holy that we detect in every living creature; that sense
of sacredness that challenges us to treat everything in a holy and
sacred way.

So, it is not the soul that gives identity or character to the body.
Every embodied existence, my own included, takes its identity and
meaning from the relational matrix. How all that is mediated is
something that should not preoccupy you too much. I myself don't
worry much about it, and frankly, I don't see why you should. Just
bask in its erotic unfolding and enjoy it as much as possible—and
make sure that everybody else shares in that erotic pleasure as well!

You mean to say . . .

AUGUSTINE: Now you're confusing us further, introducing that
   dirty word *erotic.*
JOSHUA: Hold on, Gussy, how did you get that idea into your
   head that eroticism is dirty?

AUGUSTINE: Just look at how it screwed up Adam and Eve!

JOSHUA: Gussy, I am afraid religion has taken a heavy toll on your sanity and on your humanity, and I guess it has left you in a deep state of anguish and pain. The erotic, my dear friend, is the creative impulse on which my relational matrix thrives. It is the inner dynamism of our capacity to relate. It is the loving energy through which we connect with everything in creation. Let me assure you, there is nothing dirty in this word, nor is there in the sexual energy through which humans cooperate with our desire to cocreate.

AUGUSTINE: I don't understand why you use words like *erotic* and *sex* in a public gathering. You don't know what you are arousing in people.

JOSHUA: Erotic feelings, I hope, and the more sexual they are the better, because that indicates that people are grounded in their bodies, which is precisely what delights me and the relational matrix. What's the point in incarnating bodies if bodies can't enjoy pleasure?

AUGUSTINE: I can't take any more of this; I'm going home.

JOSHUA: And when you get home, Gussy, get out of your head and just savor your body for a while; and hopefully, we'll talk again! I love you, Gussy!

AUGUSTINE: You . . . WHAT?

One of the issues that has badly damaged all our identities is this preoccupation with being in control. That is a big part of Gussy's problems with sexuality. But it is not just in the sexual realm; it has burrowed its way into every aspect of human living, leaving us often dull and weary in our engagement with life.

I'd love if you humans could explain to me why you became so preoccupied with this desire to conquer and control everything in creation? You even tried to conquer and control me. Can you explain to me why?

Kingship: The Prophetic Vision

All the material in the Christian gospel, alluding to me as King, Savior, Ruler, the Exalted One—I find it repugnant and distressing.

Some of those male followers during my earthly indwelling nearly drove me crazy. They were so addicted to power, honor, and glory! They kept missing the point and purpose of my existence, and the more I tried to enlighten them, the more frightened and scared they became.

At least I had the consolation of some women followers, who grasped what I was about. The tragedy is, of course, that history obliterated their very existence. Historians seem to be addicted to this notion of inventing heroes just as many of my male followers were. Neither I nor my relational matrix has much time for heroes.

My New Reign is not about heroes but about lovers. That's the bit the women grasped, while the male apostles just could not get the idea into their heads, never mind into their hearts. When you're heavy into conquering and controlling, it is difficult to appreciate the power and meaning of relationality.

So, who do you say that I am? At least the Gospel writers went to the trouble of recording the question. What they did not record was my frustration at never getting an authentic answer. And what hurts most of all is the emphasis Christians put on Peter's response: "You are the Christ the Son of the Living God."

Poor old Peter, my heart grieved for that guy. Most of the time, he hadn't a clue about what was going on. He dreaded anything to do with vulnerability, service, relationality, or love. He had such a poor self-image, the consequence being that he expected all the rest of us —myself included—to play power games all the time.

"You are the Christ the Son of the Living God"! What a mouthful! It certainly helps to keep me safe in a distant heaven and saves people from having to engage with my relational matrix. But what problems it has caused! And what violence has been perpetrated in my name because of statements of that nature!

Okay, let's get a few things clear. I never called myself Messiah, the Christ, Son of God. In fact, I hate titles. I do understand where these apostles—and so-called evangelists—are coming from, and I am prepared to forgive them for getting it so wrong. What amazes me is why it took Christians so long to see the fundamental flaw of the whole thing!

The flaw I refer to is the human addiction to power-posturing, a dominant feature of your past six to seven thousand years. Again let me clear up the muddle: I have nothing to do with power and I never have had. Describing me as "all-powerful" is a projection of people deluded and deceived by the patriarchal will-to-power. It has nothing to do with me; it is your confused way of understanding, and frankly it's about time you debunked the whole thing!

What you humans seem to have forgotten is that this pursuit of power belongs to only a tiny section of your great evolving story. I don't understand why you adopt it as if it were the raison d'être for everything that has transpired in your six million years on earth. Why do you judge everything through what has happened in the past few thousand years, the very time when you deviated so blatantly from your own great story?

So, let's try to get one thing straight: forget the power-mongering, and let's become united around the capacity to relate. Let's try to honor our embeddedness in the relational matrix, the primordial context of empowering love, life, and growth. That's what we're about, all of us, you and me! That's what creation is about. Please, please, please, let's go once more for the big picture and try to break loose from this crippling violent reductionism that is not only destroying the human spirit but is wreaking such havoc on everything in creation.

Believe me—hard though it may be—relationality is the ultimate clue to my identity, your identity, and the identity of everything in creation. Nothing makes sense in isolation, not even me!

Sorry to disappoint my Jewish friends, but really I am not the "I am who am." That's another man-made projection exalting me to heights where I really don't belong. "I am because we are" (*ubuntu umuntu ngabantu*) is much closer to the mark. My African brothers and sisters have known that for several millennia. Why don't you listen to them?

Okay, it sounds like I am getting into an argument here, and I am not really interested in arguments; I leave that to philosophers. I hope you have got the point about my identity, or at least you have enough to be getting on with. So we need a break. Let's sit beside a quiet stream and watch the gentle flow and realize that this is the rhythmic movement of all life, forever held in the creative embrace of my relational matrix.

Poetic Echoes . . .

"For yours is the power and honor and glory."
It bore me to tears in its frequent repeat.
"The Christ from on high, the Lord of Dominion."
Projections abound, deluded, deceived.
So, once more, I place the primordial question:
I am who you say and who do you think?
Yes, Peter was fast, compulsive as usual,
Totally concerned with his own power and pact.

In patriarchal times, we lauded our heroes
And sanctioned their power with divine attribute.
We failed to discern that the power of divine ones
Projected a hunger that was ours in its root.
It's not about power but radical service,
Suffering Servant, not Exalted Christ.
The king on the throne is replaced now forever
By relational being at the heart of the home.

Relational matrix begins new resolution
To break down the layers of power from on high.
In relating correctly, in justice and loving,
We birth forth empowerment in life that endures.
By interrelating we evoke compassion,
Declaring that all before God share a call:
To cherish and nourish, to befriend and flourish
And make all things new as our God doth implore.

The sum of relations defines our creation,
Begetting identity for all living therein.
Uniqueness is special but not separation,
Our connections bring forth the truth that we are.
Relational people relate to creation,
As the cosmos relates to a God of the heart.
A god who is centered in empowering freedom,
The core of relating for all that exists.

EPISODE THREE

The Long-awaited Messiah

NOW THAT WE HAVE CLEARED THE AIR on my identity—and yours too—let's try to get things into perspective about my connection with the Jewish people. To me the Jewish people are no more or less important than the Brazilians, the Ethiopians, the Vietnamese or those who dwell on the island of Samoa. They are all my sisters and brothers within the fellowship of my relational matrix. For me there is no prioritizing, no chosen people, and no holy nation!

Messianic Hope

MARDUK: You're a bloody traitor. You were born in Israel, circumcised, and with your family you worshiped in the synagogue.

JOSHUA: And so do people all over the world. They do so out of a particular identity that only makes sense in the context of their larger identity as planetary and cosmic creatures.

MARDUK: I am not interested in the planet or the cosmos. We are a Jewish people living in exile, looking to the mighty hand of God to rescue us and resettle us in our own land. That is what all of us—you included—should be concerned about and not all this nonsense about the planet and the cosmos.

JOSHUA: Did it ever dawn on you, Marduk, that it is your religious nationalism that has made you an exile and is keeping you trapped in the alienation of exile?

MARDUK: Adonai gave this land to our forefathers to be held in perpetuity as God's own nation.

JOSHUA: But the whole earth belongs to Adonai—how often do we pray that in the Psalms?

MARDUK: I know the whole earth belongs to Adonai, but only our nation has been chosen to bring the hope of salvation to all the others who live in darkness.

JOSHUA: Marduk, one of the tragic things that has happened to the human species is that it has lost the big picture of how I and my relational matrix operate in the world. Humans have replaced all that with this deluded version of a species grossly preoccupied with their own power.

MARDUK: So we're all wrong, and you're all right—so who the hell do you think you are?

JOSHUA: Faced with people like you, I feel like a voice crying in the wilderness, but I guess I must go on doing so, because it is for that that I was sent.

I always feel sad when I see people stuck in their ideologies. Humans are the only creatures that get stuck like this. Free will and human intelligence are wonderful gifts, but unless we use them with imagination and intuition they can be deadly liabilities. When the human mind gets stuck in its own self-perpetuated arrogance, everything becomes distorted. We lose sight of the relational matrix and the relationality on which everything in creation thrives.

I hate to think what it must feel like to spend your whole life waiting for a promised Messiah! Worse still when a whole people wait for it for a few thousand years! How could people ever become so naïve and deluded? Look around you and see the wonder and elegance of creation. Listen to its story of some thirteen billion years. Watch the emergence of organic life for some four billion years and the flourishing of your own species for six million years. And after all that, you wait for a Messiah? Why? What's going on?

NAOMI: Joshua, I love your story. It is like a breath of fresh air, but I wonder do you really understand your own people and where they are coming from?

JOSHUA: Tell me more . . .

NAOMI: You see, they have always understood that Adonai is on their side.

JOSHUA: But Adonai is on everybody's side

NAOMI: Yes, I know, please hold on a minute until I explain.
Ever since our people were exiled into Babylon, we have had the belief that we would be vindicated before our enemies, that the temple would be restored to its former glory, and

that the divine would come to dwell with us once more as God's chosen people. We were born and reared on this.

JOSHUA: Yes, I understand. Now, perhaps, the time has come to outgrow all that, to come back out of exile, not just into the land of Israel but into the whole creation in all its elegance and beauty.

NAOMI: But it seems to me that the Torah and our traditions require us first to be reconciled with our people and with our nation before we can be reconciled with the whole of creation.

JOSHUA: Naomi, did it ever strike you that it might be the exact opposite: that when you begin to come home to the whole of creation, and to the relational matrix that sustains it, then you become whole once more; reconciliation then becomes possible with all the constituent parts, nations and peoples alike.

NAOMI: I must admit, I never looked at it that way.

Beyond the Jewish Context

I found the Jewish people to be incredibly confused, and this left them feeling disenfranchised and alienated. But of course they were not the only ones feeling that way. The imperialistic approach to history has left the whole of humanity disempowered and disenfranchised. Even I myself have become the victim of that sordid process.

Since my identity belongs primarily to the relational matrix, and that matrix impregnates everything in creation, there are a few crucial issues that need to clarified and put in their right context.

1. I belong to the whole of creation and not to any one historical nation or people. Breaking the planet into segments called nations is something neither I nor my relational matrix ever wanted. That is a human invention of the culture of "divide and conquer" and has nothing to do with me and the relational matrix. For us, creation is one, undivided organism and that is how we should relate to it.

2. I have had several incarnations on planet Earth, the most notable being six million years ago when you humans first evolved.

Blimey, what an orgasmic experience that was! I will never forget the excitement and wonder I had around East Africa at that time. Probably the next most memorable were the various embodiments your researchers call the Great Earth Mother Goddess, and they happened in several parts of the planet at different times.

3. The particular incarnation that Christians believe in—it happened to be in Israel, but why people exalt that above all the others and turn it into such a crude patriarchal ideology is something I have never been able to make sense of.

4. All the religions describe my embodied state, some more overtly than others, but the problem they all suffer from is their preoccupation with divinity, which, of course, is really a preoccupation with power. Consequently, my radical presence within the creative cosmos tends to be subverted—frequently overshadowed by all the airy-fairy rhetoric about divinity.

So, yes, I did prove to be a big disappointment to the people of Israel, because I did not meet their messianic expectations. But nobody else could have met them either, because such expectations are totally unreal. For me the interesting thing about my earthly indwelling among the Jewish people is that they give good acknowledgment to my earthly status; in several of the other religious systems, they don't know what to make of it, and so it tends to be subverted or explained away in popular mythology.

From Pillars to Arches

For me the key symbols of Jewish culture were too narrow and oppressive. They seriously diminished the breadth and depth of my relational matrix. Even to this day, peoples all over the world adopt the same symbolic structures, often in a way that hinders rather than enhances the flourishing of creation and its diverse organisms. I am thinking specifically of four issues:

The Land
For the Jews of my day, land was an object of exclusiveness and power. Everybody had their "private property" with the rich having

far in excess of what they needed and the poor outrageously deprived
—even of basic necessities. That imbalance was not just because of
Roman occupation, because all patriarchal cultures treat the land
similarly. They oppress the land itself, and we all become the victims
of the internalized oppression.

For me and the relational matrix, the land is a gift to be shared
openly and freely by all. Nobody owns the land and nobody should
have exclusive rights over it; otherwise, its giftedness is undermined
and abused. And the land is one, with an incredible array of diversity enriching the oneness. Consequently the land should never have
been divided into patriarchal sections, called nations; and sooner
rather than later, I hope, you humans will once more restore the land
to its primordial unity.

The Temple

Every religion opts for sacred buildings that become exclusive and
seriously distract from the holiness of the open spaces of creation at
large. The Jewish people do not seem to have grasped a fairly obvious message: the ancient temple of Jerusalem was not destroyed by
external forces; it destroyed itself. When any institution becomes
overly self-serving, it paves the way for its self-destruction, just as is
happening to the nation state at the present time.

On occasions, sacred buildings have a purpose, but neither I nor
my relational matrix is at all happy with their extensive use. We
would prefer to see people use the sanctuary of creation itself for
prayer and worship. Our presence with you is far more apparent
and engaging when you work with us in the open spaces of the creative universe. Creation is our primary revelation for you; you
would feel so much more nourished and empowered if only you
were more meaningfully connected with creation.

The Torah

Like all the other religions, the Jewish faith evolved to a point
where law became its central value. Its followers judged themselves
and their God in terms of observance of law, which over time
became a plethora of rules and regulations almost impossible to fulfill. This led to a new spiritual combat of the holy, pure ones versus

the excluded. The whole thing became more and more disconnected from my relational matrix.

For me and the relational matrix there is basically one law, that of unconditional love; I'll talk to you about it in a short while. There is a place for law, provided it honors values that alone provide the justification for law. Even your legal people claim that the primary purpose of law is to preserve freedom, a *value* you need in order to relate more meaningfully with the relational matrix of creation.

The Family

Gee, I got myself into some deep water on this one. During my earthly indwelling, I loved my family, and I am sorry for all I put them through. It wasn't their fault, nor mine either. I had to honor the dream in my heart, and that happened to be much bigger than the family institution of that time and culture.

You see, for patriarchal cultures, family is the embryonic institution for control and subservience. Children, who in my day had no rights, learn to obey—first the head of the house (always a man), and through that structure all authority constituted in the name of patriarchal dominance. The family unit was also linked up to the control and management of land, again in an exclusive way. Although I loved the family of my Jewish incarnation, I abhorred the family system, with all the subtle power games it maintained and validated.

For me and the relational matrix, creation itself is our primary family. We all belong there in a wonderful "holarchy," where hierarchical stratifications have no place. By implication, when it comes to the human realm, we are all sisters and brothers, and what unites us is far more powerful and enduring that what divides us. We get our identity from our capacity to relate, not from our national identity, skin color, or religious affiliation. These are all aberrations put in place by the patriarchal culture of "divide and conquer."

So, lets lay to rest the Messiahs and Pariahs that have haunted us for the past six or seven thousand years. They have nothing to do with authentic faith. They belong to the culture of patriarchal domination which has nothing to do with me or my relational matrix. So, let's link arms together and leave behind that alien culture which has inflicted us with exile and estrangement, with alienation and a hell of a lot of unnecessary suffering. And let's not forget the earth itself, which also has suffered so much at the hands of patriarchal interference.

Let's leave all that behind us and embrace once more the creative hope of a new tomorrow. That's what my creative Spirit forever seeks to inspire. Let's see how she goes about it.

Poetic Echoes . . .

You wait for a better world.
What's wrong with the one you have?
You wait for a liberator
To reproach your inner slave.
You wait to see the face of God,
It's staring you in the eyes.
You wait for a better future,
And you miss today's surprise.

The waiting is a problem,
To which you love to cling.
It's all about the power games,
And the delusions that they bring.
The messianic figure—
Long before you ever knew
Irrupted in creation,
In the Spirit's vivid hue.

And the Spirit moves in freedom
Beyond the waiting and the now.
And the Spirit loves relating
When we don't control the "how."
Don't waste your time in waiting
For some God to intervene.
For God was never absent
From creation's epic scene.

EPISODE FOUR

Holy Wisdom in the Power of the Spirit

I SOMETIMES LOOK BACK over all these aeons and ponder to myself: "What a marvelous story!" And doesn't it offer us so much hope for the future! Every time things went badly pear-shaped (as you humans put it), a deep inner wisdom called forth new possibilities— a fresh breakthrough—and on ahead we go from there! Wisdom always seems to come to the rescue.

I want to tell you about that aspect of my relational matrix uniquely focused on this gift of wisdom. Christianity refers to it as the Holy Spirit and unfortunately tends to individualize and personalize it, once again deforming its true meaning.

The Horizon of Spirit

The wisdom we share in the relational matrix defies rational explanation. At one level it is the source of the relational matrix itself, begetting that interactive energy which endows the whole of creation and characterizes every relationship, human and otherwise. It is also the source that evokes various incarnations that have supported and continue to support you humans on your spiritual journey. My incarnation is just one of several that have irrupted throughout the long aeons of divine becoming. And finally, Holy Wisdom is an awakening presence that blows where she wills, generating new breakthroughs, the formative blueprints that give pattern and direction to every aspect of the evolutionary process.

The oldest and most enduring disclosure of our relational matrix is that of spirit-power. It permeates everything in creation and has done so since time immemorial. I don't understand why Christians claim that the Holy Spirit first came at an event called Pentecost about two thousand years ago. Wherever did people get that crazy notion from? The creative Spirit of my relational matrix has been totally and unambiguously present to creation for billions of years.

And the Christian church misleads a lot of people, giving the impression that as persons we receive the Holy Spirit only at baptism. So, what is the power energizing the human organism before baptism? It is the creative Spirit, totally and fully present, as in every living organism. Baptism can be, and perhaps should be, a moment of celebration of what the Holy Spirit has wrought in the world to bring a new life into being. But to suggest that there is no Holy Spirit, or some lack of Holy Spirit, before baptism—to me it sounds blasphemous!

This Spirit is the living energy, the creative vitality that stirs the waves and whispers in the wind, that warms the sun and eroticizes the moon, that vibrates in the sounds of nature, begetting novelty in every realm of creation. It scares me the way you humans try to confine my Spirit to yourselves, grossly dishonoring the pervasiveness of the Spirit in the breadth and depth of creation.

Let me also try to get something else clear! All this talk about God as *father*. Where did you get that from? Look at your sacred story over six million years; look at the unfolding of creation for over thirteen billion years. All that birthing forth, nurturing, sustaining, erotic creativity. Surely that has more to do with mothering than with fathering! And look at how your ancestors prayed and worshiped throughout the Palaeolithic era. In many ways they had it right: the motherlike God of prodigious fertility, embodied uniquely in the earth itself, because the earth belongs to the creative cosmos, infused with the Spirit of my relational matrix.

So please drop all those "father" allusions! Honestly, it has very little to do with the true essence of my relational matrix. In truth, it belongs to the patriarchal domination to which you have become so addicted. And sooner or later, you'll have to let go of all that. As a species it is really getting you nowhere!

My relational matrix is much more about a mothering energy: begetting, birthing, nurturing, sustaining, cocreating!

You mean to say . . .

SUZANNE: Excuse me, Sir, if your relational matrix is about mothering, why is it that I had to be "churched" four times after mothering my children?

JOSHUA: Suzanne, you had better ask the church that question, because I have no idea why they did such an abominable thing.

SUZANNE: The priest told me I needed to be purified—purified from what?

JOSHUA: Humans have done some strange things in the name of religion.

SUZANNE: I'm not talking about humans; I'm talking about priests. I was always told they are supposed to be God's representatives for us.

JOSHUA: Suzanne, as adult people of faith, we are all God's representatives. That's how it is and that's how it was always meant to be.

SUZANNE: Well, let me tell you something, I feel bloody angry about the whole thing.

JOSHUA: And there are times when I feel very angry about it too. If it's okay with you, Suzanne, I'd like to invite these folks to join me in praying with you for that healing we all need because of the scars that religion has caused us. Do you mind if we do that?

SUZANNE: If it helps!

JOSHUA: I am sure it will. Let us all extend our hands toward Suzanne. May you know in your heart that healing love and hope that bind up the wounds of our past and reawaken in our hearts the joy of knowing true love. Amen.

ALL: Amen.

And that is what you, too, are meant to be about. You are not slaves, servants, or observers to a process carried out on your behalf by some distant divine figurehead. I call you friends, participators, cocreators. Without you, the vision and dream of my relational matrix cannot be fully realized. My relational matrix needs you to bring to fruition the dreams we share together. I have offered you a blueprint, and it saddens me that you are so slow on the uptake.

Kinship of the Spirit

My blueprint! Oh dear, what a task it is to get that one across to you humans. As I said previously, I thought I had made it quite clear during my earthly indwelling as the Christian Jesus, but somehow people didn't grasp it. Too much mental and spiritual clutter got in the way, I guess.

Yes, I did describe this blueprint as the Kingdom of God. I know some of you are a bit baffled by the domineering, patriarchal nature of the language, but that was my way of calling people's bluff. If you attack an oppressive system directly, you can often end up empowering rather than transforming it, and there is also the risk that you yourself will get stuck in its negative karma. But if you subversively play around the perimeters and don't take it too seriously, then transformation has a much better chance of happening. In other words, "Go for poetry rather than for politics!"

Somebody described my vision as an "Upside-down Kingdom." Spot on! That's exactly what I had in mind. This craving for power, coming from the top and crippling everything on the ground—I wasn't going to go along with that. I rallied with the people and with the suffering earth. I did not try to change the power brokers—I saw no point in wasting my time and energy trying to achieve the impossible. I went instead for the option of empowerment—from the bottom up, so to speak.

Did I succeed? Well, it cost me my earthly life! The authorities began to see what I was onto, and they did not like it. They detected the potential of my dream. They destroyed me in terms of my earthly indwelling, but they could not destroy my dream because it is bigger than me. Ultimately that belongs to my relational matrix and not to me. And despite the opposition and the elimination of my earthly indwelling, the dream survived and still does. Perhaps more than anything else, what I really want to get across in my story today is to clarify once and for all what this dream is about.

You see, the Christians started translating the dream into an organization called the church. I don't know why they did that, because I never said anything about a church. I never even mentioned the word.

The Catholics are forever quoting me as having said: "Thou at Peter and upon this rock I will build my church." I have no recollection of having said that. The early Christians, who seemed more interested in their own status than in my truth, devised that claim and then attributed it to me. What a heap of racketeering!

The point I was trying to make, time and again, is that the Kingdom of God is about the world—the whole of creation—and it is much, much bigger than any specific church or religion. It is about a new way of relating with my relational matrix, in the cosmic and planetary context in which everything unfolds. And it's primary focus is twofold: (1) to name and celebrate the life-giving relationships animated by the creative Spirit; and (2) to challenge and change the destructive, life-denying relationships that inflict pain and suffering on the earth and its peoples.

Birthing Faith Communities

Does this dream require a church? I don't think so. What it does require are people united in faith communities, who are committed to this dream, and those among you exploring the notion of basic Christian communities know exactly what I mean. The holy man Paul also understood my dream when he went about Greece and Asia Minor setting up ecclesial groups—small, fluid, and flexible, committed to the task of service in the name of love and justice.

The need for meaningful community I totally support and endorse, but ecclesiastical organization is something I have huge problems with. All that bureaucracy and pomp, along with the rhetoric around control and moralizing—it has achieved so little in creating the new world envisaged in the Kingdom of God. What is particularly disturbing is the way in which women have been oppressed and ostracized. They have always been the backbone of the Christian story, right from the initial proclamation of resurrection hope, but their vision, giftedness, and resilience have never been honored. In fact, they have often been brutally crushed in a way that is deeply alien to my will for humanity and to the vision of new life born out of my relational matrix.

So, cocreators, are you with me this time? As people imbued with the living Spirit, let's make a fresh start; let's get the vision clear. We are all about the Kingdom of God, religious or otherwise, that new world order marked by right relationships of justice, love, compassion, and liberation. That's the heart and soul of everything. It's all about getting relationships right, in the sense of aligning them more explicitly with the fullness of life that my relational matrix engenders in every sphere of creation.

I began this episode explaining the role of Holy Spirit, the Wisdom power of my relational matrix and of everything in creation. This Spirit permeates everything and is reflected in every form of birthing forth, even amid the paradoxes and contradictions of life. The Spirit evidences a fundamental Wisdom that permeates and undergirds everything in creation. Your human intelligence is derived from this Wisdom.

The problem, of course, is that humans often forget the source of their enlightenment, and this can lead to many problems. The Spirit's Wisdom is indeed very powerful, but humans need to learn how to channel it appropriately. There is a dark side to the Spirit's Wisdom, reflecting the paradox of creation/destruction, which characterizes the universe at every level. As you humans know, too much of a good thing can itself overwhelm or oppress. We need to be aware of the mind and intellect through which we appropriate and assimilate the Spirit's Wisdom.

The scriptures of many traditions talk about *testing the Spirits.* Any of us can be self-deluded, so we need to be open to the gift and challenge of shared wisdom. Wisdom needs to be exposed to reflective consideration and genuine dialogue. Part of the problem is that wisdom tends to be monopolized by the academics in society, whereas the Wisdom of my relational matrix belongs as much to the simple as to the sophisticated. Frequently too much learning is a real barrier to discernment.

So, on the one hand, you humans need to relish and cherish the abundance of wisdom with which you are imbued, within and without. And, second, you need to set in place channels for engaging with Wisdom, so that you appropriate it authentically and use it creatively for the service of my Kingdom on earth.

I suggest we might need to meditate for a while to take all that in. Let's move into a silent space . . . !

Poetic Echoes . . .

You ask for the Spirit to come from on high
And you pray for the wisdom you need.

And you hope 'twill be given to help you along
To unravel your meaning and creed.

But the creed you espouse disturbs me a lot,
Distorted and prone to mislead.
With Father and Son controlling the plot
I'm not sure what the Spirit can wield.

The Spirit in fact is the one who comes first
Impregnating all that is new.
Shaping and molding what time can bring forth
A-flourishing erotic hue.

The life force of Spirit is ancient and new
And ageless in restless content.
The first face of God our ancestors knew
In creation's relentless intent.

Beholding her wisdom at work in the land
With symbols of water and flame.
She blows where she wills, enkindling anew,
The sparkle to form and name.

This spiritual power that permeates all,
Evoking a wisdom so rare.
Yet, deep in our hearts she also abides
Assuring our freedom and fare.

EPISODE FIVE

Loved Unconditionally

I LOVE MOUNTAINS! In fact, I love everything in creation, but mountains are very special for me. What I love about mountains is the panoramic view. There is so much to be seen from a mountaintop: valleys, rivers, lakes, fields and forests, creatures and their habitats. The whole thing weaves into a kind of tapestry, and one begins to ask: What or Who is behind it all?

Now this is the beginning of faith—true faith. Faith is about getting the right question, not necessarily the right answer. And nature is great for awakening questions; in fact, nature can evoke the questions in a way that nothing else can. In the vast panorama of nature, cosmic life is constellated and concentrated. Come home to nature and you begin to understand my relational matrix. Come home to nature and you come home to the heart that pulsates throughout the vast cosmos.

Loved into Loving

Rightly, indeed, you humans discern the heart as the symbol of love. Creation is a symphony of love. Everything from galaxies to planets, land masses to people, rhinos to turtles—all are given in love. All adorn the landscape because my relational matrix loves beauty and we offer beauty in a spirit of unconditional love. Assuredly, the offer is made in freedom, and that often leads to chaos and even pain—but I'll come to that later.

For now, let's stay with love! You humans are forever glamorizing the power of love. You do it in songs and sonnets, films and advertising, glitzy images, and pornographic lore. But I notice it is always something to be worked for, something to be earned—for which a price has to be paid. Consequently, you always tend to end up licking the wounds of love forgotten, or love betrayed, or love not honored in one form or another.

And so much of your religion is about trying to convince me that I should love you in some better way. You pile up penance and prayer, novena and intercession, trying to convince me that I should love you. And the more you pile on the pressure, the more disenchanted and disillusioned you seem to become.

The Incredible Bit!

Okay, let's get to the point. My relational matrix and I love everything in creation *unconditionally*. Got it? That's how it always has been with us and that's how it always will be. Ridiculous, isn't it? especially for those who somehow don't get the message.

That's how it is folks! Don't waste your time trying to convince us that we should love you! We're ahead of you on that one. We have always loved you, and loved you unconditionally, which for many of you, I guess, is the incredible bit. Assuredly, we know all about your sins and failures and transgressions, but despite all those we still love you—*unconditionally!*

You mean to say . . .

VOICE FROM THE CROWD: So, if it is as simple as that, what's the point in following God's way at all.

JOSHUA: Good question! And by the way, just note, I did not say it is *simple!* That is one of your big problems; you humans simplify love by making it conditional on what should and should not be done. You seek love and offer love, but always with conditions attached. Therefore, the notion of unconditional love is a bit of an unknown quantity among you, and hence my reason for emphasizing the point.

VOICE: But you are telling us something different from the commandments of our religion.

JOSHUA: No, I am speaking to you about the commandment that lies beneath all the commandments. In fact, I am speaking about the very thing that is at the basis of all meaning, human and divine.

VOICE: How is it that we have not been told this before now?

JOSHUA: Because the true message has been lost in the clutter of rules and regulations.

VOICE: But all our teachers and holy men tell us that we can't serve Adonai unless we obey his rules and laws.

JOSHUA: "His" rules and laws? Sounds like you believe in the ruling judge from on high! Sorry to disappoint you, my good friend, but that guy does not even exist!

VOICE: (pause), Oh, I don't know what to say. It all sounds so confusing—and this unconditional bit, it throws me completely! It's almost too good to be true.

JOSHUA: How right you are!

Let's take this issue step by step: I and my relational matrix love unconditionally everything in creation. Just take my word for it for the moment, and also for the fact that we will continue to love you unconditionally no matter how much of a mess you make of life.

a. So, the first thing we suggest is that you trust us (me and the relational matrix)—unconditionally—and take the risk that all will turn out well. That sounds a bit crazy, doesn't it? But as you shall see in a minute the crazy bit is more about you than about me.

b. Now, if you begin to buy into my unconditional love, the chances are you'll understand the next step. This is the BIG one: are you ready?

c. If you are loved unconditionally (which you are), then you too must learn to love unconditionally. Now that's the bit where the eyelids begin to droop, and as the Gospel says about the rich young man: he went away sad! He couldn't take on the challenge.

You mean to say . . .

BARAK: But I have worked hard and put up these buildings with the best materials I could purchase. I have to be responsible about my finances and all this money my grand-uncle passed on to me.

JOSHUA: Barak, you can't take it with you. What you have achieved is great, but now the challenge is to use it to make life great for others, particularly those with so little.

BARAK: Sir, a lot of those fellows would not be poor if they got up off their asses and did a decent day's work.

JOSHUA: Barak, judge not, and you will not be judged!

d. The point is not about service to me and my relational matrix. We never suggested that you should reciprocate the love to us. To be honest with you, we are not particularly worried whether you love *US* or not. What we are concerned about is that you love life unconditionally, just as we love it unconditionally. It is not about loving us; it is about being in solidarity with us and with the love we seek to share.

e. The whole point of our existence, and yours too, is that together we cocreate a world of unconditional loving. You have been good at it for much of your earthly evolving journey. This past eight thousand years have been a particularly bad patch for you humans. You really need to let go of that addiction to power and start loving and trusting once more.

Calling Forth the Adult!

Yes, the song says it beautifully: "Love changes everything!"—especially unconditional love. Under the influence of this new way of relating, hierarchical ways of being no longer hold any meaning. Ours is a dispensation of mutually empowering partnership, one in which we and you work together for the cocreation of new life, hope, and promise. Codependency, based on parent–child modeling, has no place in a world governed by unconditional love. A new network of relationships is evoked in which *adults* relate interdependently with each other and with the relational matrix.

Love is the fundamental dynamism of all religion, but sadly it is the very feature compromised by religion itself. I said that to one of the Pharisees during my earthly indwelling, but he responded as if the whole thing was a sick joke!

You mean to say . . .

ELEAZER: I never heard such nonsense in all my life. Adonai gave us commandments and will love us only if we obey them. Every child has been taught that since he was knee-high.

JOSHUA: And what has it achieved for you? Why are your children full of fear and guilt?

ELEAZER: Because they are trying to earn God's love and forgiveness.

JOSHUA: But why?

ELEAZER: In order to inherit eternal life.

JOSHUA: But eternal life is all around you, man; look at the lilies of the fields, look at the birds of the air; they trust in unconditional love, so why don't you?

ELEAZER: Please sir, don't be comparing me with lilies and birds.
I am a human being with an immortal soul, for which I am
responsible before God. Lilies and birds don't have souls,
and perhaps you don't either.

JOSHUA: You have it all wrapped up, haven't you! And the thing
about unconditional love is that you can't wrap it; it thrives
on freedom and creativity.

You humans tend to construe the power of love as you fabricate
most other things in life. You quantify and measure wisdom in your
insatiable desire for control. This desire to control is the milestone
around your necks choking to death your capacity for love and creativity.

You need to learn anew the capacity for trust arising from the
benevolence of unconditional love. Everything in life is bestowed as
gift for your delight and well-being, but so much has been desecrated,
dishonored and maligned by the hunger for power and control.

Creation itself groans with the anguish and pain of unloving people, torturing the earth they no longer seem capable of loving. Well,
my friends, without the earth, you are worth nothing. The earth is
the planetary womb of sustenance, growth, and creative potential.
Healthy, wholesome humans need a healthy, wholesome earth, to
love joyfully and attain the fulfillment God intends for all. It is folly
to yearn for union with my relational matrix until you first bond
closely with creation itself. The depth of our love for creation is the
barometer of your love for me and for the relational matrix.

I hope this has clarified the nature of my relational matrix. Love
is the primordial force for bringing everything into existence and for
holding it in being. Love is the pregnant and formative power for all
possibility. Possibilities unfold through interdependent relationships,
the most enduring of which is my relational matrix, concretized—
from a Christian point of view—in the New Reign of God.

In the context of God's New Reign, my individual identity—my
earth-bound indwelling—is molded and put at the service of relational becoming. The same is true for you and indeed for every
organism in creation. That process of becoming, while often random
and chaotic, is ultimately sourced by love, and with the ascendancy

of unconditional love, life moves inexorably and irreversibly toward healing, wholeness, and new life.

Let's take a break! Anybody who feels up to it, please join me on a visit to St. Giles Hospice in Bulawayo. I want to spend some time with the people dying of HIV/AIDS.

They, too, have stories to tell and a lot of love to share!

Poetic Echoes . . .

We're good at laying down the conditions
And we judge by how well we achieve.
We must measure up and get to the top
Nothing less will appease those in charge.

Forever we're judging how well we can do
And ourselves we oft judge through the others.
It's a game of no-win, amid failure and sin,
Subverting the grace of true freedom.

It's a human concoction, perverted and false,
A projection we force on the Godhead.
Conditions we lay for a ransom to pay
To the one who's outwitted our scheming.

There are no conditions for divine plenitude
For grace has demolished the broker.
A paradigm shift, both ancient and swift
Releases a new liberation.

Unconditionally loved we always have been.
The ridiculous grace of abundance.
And the same we must show to friend and to foe,
And that is the challenge so daunting.

It's all about trust and the risk that's involved
Beyond the control of exertion.
Empowered by God's grace, this challenge we face.
We have power to transform the nations.

EPISODE SIX

I Love Stories

I HOPE YOU NEVER let your children go to bed at night without telling them a good story. Children love stories and so do adults! The big problem we have today is that we have an abundance of children's stories but a dearth of adult stories.

And that leads to a further problem—that many of our children's stories are not very wholesome in terms of the big picture of life and the bigger reality of creation. Many children's stories arise from fantasies of repressed power. Women are often depicted as demons, and the victor is nearly always a male.

So, friends, we have a big piece of work to do around stories and storytelling! But for now, I just want to stay with the stories you have accumulated around my earthly indwelling. Some wonderful stories there, but again, many of them have been badly distorted even by the holy men who wrote and edited them.

Stories That Stretch

One of my favorites is what my friend Luke calls the story of the Good Samaritan.

I remember it well—the evening I was attacked on the road from Jerusalem down to Jericho. They ran away with my outer garment and left me half naked, but at least they did not beat me up as they often did to others.

Actually, it was not long after that when I came across Ishmael lying on the side of the same road. Poor old soul, he had endured a terrible battering. I remember particularly the gash under his left eye, and since it was the time of the rainy season, there was mud and muck everywhere. Let me tell you, it was a messy sight.

Ishmael was aching, weak, and weepy, so he was going to be categorized as "half-dead." That was one of the categories of ritual impurity adopted by my religion. Just then, this group came along, all fellows, and some of them were wearing religious attire. Clever so-and-so's, they always traveled in groups. They knew it was safer. I recognized Raguel. He was the one who had confronted me the previous week about healing on a Sabbath day. I'll tell you something: he read out this list of what you could and could not do on the Sabbath. I was left wondering if I could even urinate! I also recognized Jacob—he was one of the Levites. Well, he looked at me with a frown on his face—you could almost crack glass with it!

The whole group of them walked by on the other side, as if poor old Ishmael and I did not even exist. I thought to myself, "Isn't it disgusting what religion has done to us?" Just because a poor old soul is bleeding and half-dead, he is labeled impure and treated as a total outsider. Where in the name of God did they get that crap from? Nothing ever has been, or could be, excluded from my relational matrix.

Anyhow, to hell with them all. I stayed there with Ishmael, and tried to give him what nurturance and hope I could. Rachel and her two children came along with a donkey laden with shopping and some furniture. Ishmael sipped some juice and was able to munch a little fruit—and I'll tell you something, I was damn glad to have a nibble myself. Just as we were considering how best to get Ishmael on to the mule so that we could get him some badly needed medical help, along came Roderick.

Stories That Include

Now, I had never seen this guy before, and I wasn't sure what we were dealing with. I suspected he was a Samaritan, and as it turns out I was right. And I'll tell you something: it was incredible what happened. Apparently, he worked as a paramedic, but he did not have any equipment with him. So down on his knees he goes, examining the wounds and offering kind and loving words. I couldn't believe my eyes. Those Samaritans and Jews hated the very mention of each other's names. That this could be happening baffled me and truly delighted my heart, as I knew it would be such a joy for my relational matrix.

And this guy—he told me his name was Roderick—was not interested in any half-measures. Ishmael needed hospital care and he was going to get it, and nothing short of the best was Roderick going to procure. So, up on to the road he goes and waves down a big truck.

A greedy old sod, the truck driver wanted two hundred denarii to take Ishmael to hospital, which was a mere twenty-minute drive. But Roderick didn't seem to be that worried about money; all he was concerned about was the suffering plight of Ishmael. So between us we got him into that truck and off they went.

A few days later I visited the hospital myself and found Ishmael devouring a wholesome meal of lentils and humus. Needless to say, I had a nibble myself; it looked so appetizing I just couldn't resist. Ishmael was so appreciative of Roderick, who made sure he was given the best of everything with all expenses paid. I tell you, folks, I find this story so exemplary and incredible, I just love telling it. It breaks down so many barriers, demolishing all this propaganda about inclusion and exclusion. Roderick probably never heard me or anyone else speak of the Kingdom of God, but let me assure you that as far as my relational matrix is concerned, Roderick lives and promotes the values of the Kingdom of God in a way that leaves many religionists limping far behind.

Roderick knows what working for right relationships is all about. That, too, is what I am about, and what my relational matrix has been about for several billions of years. Roderick has a very special place in my heart.

One of the Pharisees, a self-righteous twit, was trying to catch me out one day. They are forever doing that; they just can't help it; it is the result of all the indoctrination they have been put through. Anyhow, he was quoting from the Book of Exodus about love of God and love of neighbor, and he went on and on and on. Then all of a sudden, he sneaks in a another innocent question loaded with malicious intent: "And who is my neighbor?" I felt like saying: "Well, what a stupid question!" "Right," I said to myself, "let's take this smart prankster for a bit of a ride."

I knew the answer he wanted, but I don't answer direct questions—it's not good for people's imaginations—so I told him the story of Ishmael and Roderick. Well, wasn't he disgusted, especially when we came to the bit about the Samaritan. By the time I was finished, he was boiling over with resentment. He turned around and walked away—and I shouted after him:

You mean to say . . .

JOSHUA: You go and do the same, mate!

NATHAN: Are you out of your mind? How dare you tell me, a person of your own religion, to flout and disrespect our faith!

JOSHUA: Nathan, what we need is love, not religiosity; we have had religion for centuries, and where has it got us?

NATHAN: It has kept us right before God, you stupid idiot.

JOSHUA: But God is love, and if you don't love the person that you see, and meet and touch each day, how can you love the God you don't see.

NATHAN: We see all things through faith, and we don't need a Samaritan-loving thug like you coming along and trying to tell us that we should do things differently.

JOSHUA: Nathan, before you were ever called a Jew, and Roderick was called a Samaritan, you shared a common flesh and a common spirit. There are things that unite every one of us that go far beyond the things that divide and separate us.

NATHAN: You know something, you are a pure traitor to your faith. You have betrayed the one, true God for all these pagan infidels, and you don't seem to have the slightest bit of shame for what you are doing.

JOSHUA: I know what I am doing, and I know that the planet and the universe support what I am doing.

NATHAN: The planet and the universe? What have they got to do with God? Now we really know you are possessed!

JOSHUA: I guess, Nathan, we will have to agree to differ; we clearly belong to two different worlds and see things very differently.

NATHAN: We can differ as much as we like, but I know that I am right and that you are wrong, and that's what makes the difference before God.

Well, you know, every generation has had its evangelicals, and there is not much any of us can do with them. In their own eyes, they are right and that is it. But, folks, let's not forget that we inhabit a planet and belong to a universe that is vast, wide, and full of undiscovered truth. It beautifully radiates the deep richness of my relational matrix, which eludes so many of these folks that get overattached to religion. They become so addicted to the God stuff that they become blind to the divine elegance of creation staring them in the face.

Anyhow, where was I? Oh, yes, the story . . . Sorry folks, I got a bit distracted there. Please be careful not to get too wrapped up with these Nathan guys. I know they are very needy people, and we should try to show them as much love as possible. But in the end, they can wear you out, and that is not on! There is too much work for love and justice waiting to be done. So, let's get back to the storytelling!

Stories That Make a Difference

A good story is worth its weight in gold. Stories liberate the imagination, enflame the soul and awaken inner resources to resist those who crush the human spirit and devastate the living planet. What I want you to note more than anything else is the inclusiveness of my stories. For my relational matrix, there is no inside or outside. Everything is *in;* everything and everybody is included. It could not be otherwise in the realm of unconditional love.

That does not mean that everything is perfect; I'm not even perfect myself. Perfection is one of those moralistic hang-ups that drives people crazy, and of course it is easier for the dominant culture to control people when we declare them to be crazy. Perfection is a kind of ideology that halts growth and generates addictions. More dangerously still, it creates elites of power and privilege who undermine the very meaning of my Kingdom.

That's why I tell that wonderful story about the two people in the temple. There are actually two versions of that story, and typically, only the male version has survived. But I prefer the female one, because it is much more inclusive, provocative, and liberating. A noble elder is praying in the temple, basically thanking Adonai that he has had a good run at virtuous living and was able to observe the law in minute detail. I think I'd find that quite boring, and to be honest with you, I don't see what it has to do with my relational matrix. Anyhow, he seems to have found meaning in it, so let him at it!

So there he is, absorbed in divine ecstasy—I'm not sure myself what that is all about—and praying for the grace to continue in the good path. And into the back walks Sarah. It was I who suggested that she should go in there, although she was likely to get one hell of a lambasting for having done so. In some cases, women were not supposed to be in the precincts of the temple, never mind inside it. And it was publicly known that Sarah had what we call "a reputation." She hung around street corners and sold her body to make money. She said she had to do it to survive and feed her two children.

So there she was at the back of the temple, feeling as low as the sinking *Titanic*, her shaggy, unkempt hair trailing down over her breasts and tears seeping out between the closed eyelids as she mutters to herself: "O Adonai, what a fucking mess I have made of my life." She didn't stay long—she felt she had no right to be there. "Why not," I asked.

You mean to say . . .

SARAH: I know you are trying to care, Josh, but listen, I am a sinful woman; I'd rather be left alone.

JOSHUA: But why, Sarah, what's to be gained by that?

SARAH: I have been a sinner all my life, and that's how it will remain; I just can't get it right.

JOSHUA: But, Sarah, I came to call the sinners, not the just ones. I can work with sinners, but I can't stomach all those righteous ones.

SARAH: You can work with the ones that will make some effort; I'm so fucked-up I don't even know where to start.

JOSHUA: It doesn't matter how fucked-up you are, you are still special and unique. You just need a little bit more loving!

SARAH: Please Josh, don't mention that word *love* to me; it drives me crazy.

JOSHUA: That's my whole point, Sarah, despite all the mess you have been in, you are still a lovable person, and let me ask you something: did it ever dawn on you that those who have struggled most with loving are exactly the ones who know what real love is all about?

SARAH: Now, Josh, to me that sounds a bit like the bullshit those guys called psychologists come out with.

JOSHUA: But it's true, Sarah. The heart that has been pierced and broken is the heart that is open to receive the pain of every other broken heart.

SARAH (*long pause*): Yes! That makes a bit more sense. I like that, but I guess that takes a whole lifetime to achieve.

JOSHUA: Maybe! But the work of a lifetime never happens until we decide to start somewhere, and when we're down in the dumps, that is as good a place as any to start.

SARAH: I have tried so often, I don't want to go through all that again.

JOSHUA: I'll tell you what, let's go over to Rebecca's place, and we'll have something to eat. That's a more homey place to continue our conversation.

I saw the first smile on Sarah's face that day. Why wouldn't she smile! Rebecca's was the place where the prostitutes used to gather before going out for a night's business. Even though I didn't approve of what they were doing, they welcomed me in, because they trusted me as a caring friend. As Sarah and I were strutting down the road, arm in arm, well you should see the faces of the Pharisees. I guess I drove their blood pressure to rocketing levels.

You mean to say . . .

AMOK: There he goes again, parading himself with sinners and prostitutes, and he has the bloody cheek to claim that he is of God.

MALTHUS: Listen, colleagues, the sooner we get rid of that bastard, the better for all of us. He is leading the people astray and he is a total scandal to our nation.

JOSHUA: What about a bit of love and forgiveness for a change instead of the same old crap, day in and day out?

MALTHUS: Only God can forgive sins, and you certainly are not of God.

VOICE FROM THE CROWD: And how often, Sir, must I forgive, . . . seven times?

JOSHUA: Seventy times seven, my good friend, is a bit closer to the mark.

AMOK: He is blaspheming. He is claiming to do what only God can do. He deserves to die.

JOSHUA: You whitewashed sepulchres, you wait and see . . . wisdom will be proved right by her deeds!

Oh yes, I heard what they said; scarcely a day went by when I didn't hear the same empty rhetoric. As for forgiveness, if we can't forgive each other, how can we ever hope to receive forgiveness from creation and from the divine. Anyhow, I was enjoying the erotic company of Sarah, so I wasn't going to get ensnared in all their heady diatribe. I had to honor the liberation of new life required of me by my relational matrix. And Rebecca's house sounded like a good place to do just that.

Poetic Echoes . . .

Once upon a time—so the story goes,
Round it comes again as the wisdom grows.
Every child enamored and the adult, too,
Likes a damn good story to nourish life anew.

Stories load our meaning and release our search,
Help to make connections with our living earth.
Stories keep evolving, parabolic space,
Keeping us a-grounded in every age and place.

Creation tells a story, replete in night and day,
Each unfolding moment illuminates the way.
Our desire for story we appropriate,
From creation's own desire ever to narrate.

And God's plan for creatures—that's a story, too,
All the great religions add their rendezvous.
Mystics through the ages also tell the tale
Amazing grace and bounty ever do prevail.

Jesus told us stories, a New Reign open wide
Expanding closed horizons, divisions cast aside.
These are stories of the future, inaugurating hope
And stretching imagination to the limits of our scope.

Humans have a tendency the story to subvert.
We make it safe and undisturbed; its truth we oft pervert.
We need to keep wide open the landscape of the new.
If we close the parable we no longer see what's true.

Episode Seven

Wisdom Has Set Her Table

BY THE TIME we got to the house (what the locals called the brothel), I was famished. And the folks there knew that. Why wouldn't they? They knew I loved food. And they had long got over the shock that I shared food liberally and joyfully with everybody, even with so-called people of disrepute.

They knew I did not approve of the sex trade, and, to be fair, many of them did try to change their ways. I could see it was not easy for them in a regime where the Romans imposed heavy taxes and the Jews robbed people for religious favors. I knew they were not prostituting for pleasure but out of dire economic necessity. Changing personal behavior was one thing, which several tried to do. Changing the corrupt system that drove many to behave immorally would take a concerted effort and a depth of wisdom that the human species has scarcely yet discovered.

Hospitality beyond Boundaries

What I like about Rebecca's house—the den of iniquity as the righteous ones called it—was its glowing sense of community. It was not just the prostitutes that gathered there. It was a favorite haunt for sinners, tax collectors, the blind, the lame, outcasts of every type.

Nobody was ever turned away from that house. Some of my best healing took place at Rebecca's, and it was not just me bringing healing to others—we all helped to heal one another. After a few hours at Rebecca's, you were sure to depart a good deal more wholesome than when you entered.

Once I invited Peter, James, and John to come along with me to Rebecca's. Holy smoke, what a furor that caused! As you might guess, poor old Peter was horrified and gave me a big mouthful about people losing their virginity! Anyhow, James and John came along; they were scared out of their skin and I guess were damn glad to get out of the place: Shortly after, this conversation transpired:

JAMES AND JOHN: Rabbi, we met this mad fellow the other day, possessed up to his eyeballs, and we desperately tried to expel the evil spirit and we could get nowhere.

JOSHUA: I suspect your creative energies were too scattered. You were not centered. For many of these challenges you need more prayer and fasting

PETER: Prayer and fasting? Well, you're the smart one to talk about prayer and fasting. What do you know about fasting, you spend most of your time feasting.

JOSHUA: Peter, you won't have the bridegroom with you always. There is a time for fasting, but more importantly a time for feasting!

PETER: I think this feasting is getting out of hand, especially the kind of company you keep. I don't blame the Pharisees for being so scandalized.

JOSHUA: Are you thinking of joining them, Peter?

PETER: Rabbi, you have the words of eternal life, and precisely for that reason, we expect you to behave in a more respectable way, with dignity and with authority!

JAMES AND JOHN: We agree; the whole thing gets a bit worrying at times. You seem to have more time for all those women than you have for us.

JOSHUA: Well then, come and join in with me and the women— we don't exclude anybody.

PETER: But how can we join in when you are always hanging around the brothel. I have to think of my wife and family and my marriage vows. If the in-laws heard that I was consorting with that bunch, there would be holy murder.

JOSHUA: Well, then, invite the in-laws along.

JAMES AND JOHN: You don't take us seriously, do you?

JOSHUA: Maybe the problem is that you take yourselves too seriously. How can you enjoy the exuberance of creation and the delightfulness of my relational matrix if you are forever scrutinizing everything I say and do.

PETER: Because we expect you to act in accordance with God.

JOSHUA: And tell me, Peter, when did you become an expert on what God is all about. I don't fully understand the divine myself, so how could you?

JAMES AND JOHN: But we're chosen by God aren't we and we're meant to be special.

JOSHUA: In the eyes of my relational matrix everybody—and every thing in creation—is special.

PETER: But when you called us as special ones, I thought you gave us special power—you know the kind of power that nobody else could possibly have.

JOSHUA: Gosh, Peter, how did you get things so wrong? Peter, the whole enterprise is about service for empowerment; it has nothing to do with power as you understand it.

You know, this is what happened so often. I was onto something of real importance, like trying to empower Sarah at Rebecca's place, and I get ensnared in these bizarre conversations with those male followers of mine, and honestly, we lose perspective on what really matters. It suddenly dawned on me that I needed to take stock of myself; this was happening too often, and a lot of precious time was being wasted in futile arguments about the rights and wrongs of religion. Let's get back to Rebecca's place.

It was the meals we shared there more than anything else that stand out in my mind. That was actually the reason why I and so many others felt so much at home there. We totally ignored all the prohibitions about table fellowship—who should be included or excluded, how far up to the elbow you have washed, and all that jazz! We just ignored the whole thing. For my part, I knew my relational matrix could not stomach all that exclusion and believe you me, those ordinary folk—many of whom were desperately impover-ished—knew instinctively that what we were doing was right.

Feed My People!

I'll tell you another thing—which is not recorded in the Christian Gospels—nobody left that house without carrying a food parcel for those we knew to be in need. We weren't a pack of self-indulgent gluttons—something we were often accused of being—we were heavily into inclusion and thought about everybody in need.

I love those stories in the Gospels about the feeding of the big crowds, five hundred, four thousand, often several hundreds. Scholars waste a lot of time and energy trying to figure out the magic that I worked on those occasions. Let me tell you that if you had been at Rebecca's place as often as I was, and had experienced the way we shared food there, you would have no problem understanding the feeding of the crowds.

Some days in that house there was not a morsel of food in the larder, but we all chipped in, shared what we had, and collected a few dimes and denarii to buy the extra we needed. By the time we had eaten and were replenished, amazingly, there was always some left over for the poor folks in the hamlets and barrios. After that, I knew in my heart, that there always would be enough food—and more than enough to see nobody go empty!

What hurts me more than anything else in your world today is the mass starvation that so many innocent people have to endure. It tears my heart to pieces. There is so much food on this planet it could feed the current population ten times over—if only those in charge would ensure fair distribution. This bartering of food as a tool of trade and brutal economics sickens me to death. I only wish that those who foster these gross aberrations could have visited Rebecca's brothel—even once. Then they wouldn't be hoarding food in these brutal games of greed, consumerism, and oppression.

One evening I left Rebecca's place feeling well nourished in my body, but emotionally it had been quite a draining time. I needed to be alone so that I could reconnect with my relational matrix. So I escaped to a quiet place and found myself pondering that wonderful passage in Proverbs 9:1–6. As I recall it, it goes like this:

Wisdom has built herself a house, she has erected her seven pillars;
She has slaughtered her beasts, prepared her wine; she has laid her
    table.
She has dispatched her maidservants and proclaimed from the city
    heights:
"Those who are ignorant let them step this way."
To the fool she says: "Come and eat my bread, drink the wine I have
    prepared!
Leave your folly and you will live, walk in the ways of perception.

Nurtured in Wisdom

Wisdom Sophia—the wise and holy energy of my relational matrix!
Dabhar is the word they use in the Hebrew. I am puzzled as to why
my friend John describes it as *Logos*—one of those Greek, individualistic, heady concepts, almost the exact opposite of Sophia. It also
baffles me that scripture scholars try to situate my earthly indwelling
in the context of the kingly and prophetic traditions of the Hebrew
scriptures, but they rarely link me to the great wisdom tradition.
Why do scholars always situate me on the side of the winner, and
not of the loser? On the side of power and not with the powerless?
I never had much time for winners, especially those who win at the
expense of others. As for kings—forget about them. They are the
very antithesis of what my relational matrix is about.

But Wisdom Sophia, yes! That is the context that can help both
you and me to get things right. And I have no problem with the fact
that Wisdom in the Hebrew scriptures tends to be personified as a
woman: Lady Wisdom. I think that is wonderful. After all, for thirty
thousand years, you humans related with my relational matrix
through the medium of the great Earth Goddess. And lest you forget: nobody went hungry in those days; nobody was excluded, and
few people lorded it over others.

Then all of a sudden it dawned on me: Earth Goddess–Lady Wisdom–Rebecca. These are all personifications of the same fundamental story. Exuberant, vivacious women, blessed with prodigious
fertility and explosive erotic energy. The energy of my relational
matrix runs through their veins.

Of course, let's not forget the Black Madonna, the mothering channel through which my incarnational presence was born on the earth. Where, may I ask, did you humans get this bizarre notion of a white, European, virginal figure? Such a convoluted concoction! As if you were not satisfied with the European colonization of the African people, the Asians, and the Latinos, you also try to colonize and make me out to be the progeny of a desexualised, sanitized, caricature of European subservience. What has that got to do with wisdom in any sense of the word? That is the ignorance of oppression in its most blatant fashion, and it makes me very angry and disillusioned with you humans.

Forgive me for that outburst, but it really does enrage me, and of course the sin needs to be named in terms of where it really belongs, namely, to patriarchal male dominance, so self-inflated and self-deluded that it ends up not just oppressing humans themselves but is desperately trying to control and manipulate everything I also represent. More than anybody else, it is the patriarchs that need to hear the words: "Your ways are not my ways."

Come on folks, let's get rid of all that anthropocentric and addictive desire for power. It has nothing to do with me and never had. Let's repent, wake up to the bigger picture and learn to live creatively with the New Reign of my relational matrix. You Christians have wasted enough opportunities over the past two thousand years. It is about time that you take seriously the truth that will set you free.

Poetic Echoes . . .

Cruel the craving of the child with empty aching bowel.
Cruel the world that robs that child for economic prowl.
Abundant goodness bloated to expedite the hoard
While millions curse the hoarder,
In their plight!

A-cursed be the money-men who rob us of our rights.
A-cursed be the powerful ones with greedy selfish sights.
There is enough for everyone and God designed it so.
So why the hoarding and the waste?
A sickening sight!

The Churches too are guilty of a table split in two.
Those who are deemed worthy and the others left to rue.
But I never closed the table—to the sinner or the slave,
So, who the hell do you think you are?
Pontificating trite!

I'm angry with injustice, for I've been victimed too,
I set an open table with abundance to imbue.
I celebrate the gift of food and want all to have enough.
So feed my people, one and all—in their
Inalienable right!

Episode Eight

A New Commandment I Give You!

So, YOU SEE how blessed you humans are. You are intimately linked with my relational matrix, loved unconditionally, endowed with the wise Holy Spirit, and on top of all that you have the laws of your faith to support you on the way! Yes, I can see a few of you looking a bit perplexed when I mentioned "the laws of your faith." I don't blame you, I am quite perplexed myself with what you have done with my law.

Basically there is only one law, and you all learned it as little children in your own homes: "Love God and love the neighbor." And you can only do the one by doing the other! The holy man Moses broke the law into ten parts. Some bits are fine; more are just put in place to satisfy the ruling powers of the day. The danger with emphasizing the ten is that you forget the basic one on which all ten are based and without which neither the ten nor the ten hundred will make any sense.

Of course the primary purpose of all law is to protect freedom. Unfortunately, the religions seem to have largely forgotten that fact, and because they have forgotten it, they tend to make laws at a ridiculous rate, imposing burdens on peoples' shoulders that are impossible to carry, and duties that are impossible to fulfill. You then end up thinking of me and my relational matrix as a supreme lawmaker. Nothing could be farther from the truth.

So, let's get back to basics. The law behind all laws is the unconditional love I spoke about earlier. In the religion of my earthly indwelling that translated into love God and love your neighbor. My big problem about that translation is that it says nothing about creation. If we don't love the creation we see around us, then we can't really love the divine or the human in any meaningful way. Then we are left with the rather incestuous tendency of turning the great commandment into something very holy for our private lives, forgetting that its primary purpose is for public behavior and not for private devotion.

To face the consequences of the great commandment, we need to get rid of the legalities that get in the way. In my earthly indwelling, people were crucified trying to observe three predominant legalities, which continue to reverberate even to this day: first, the patron–client arrangement; second, purity laws; and third, the patriarchal family system.

All these arrangements were put in place as if they belonged to me and my relational matrix, but I never heard of them until I came here for my earthly indwelling. They have nothing to do with me and the relational matrix. They belong to the dominant power system that is desperately trying to get control over everything you humans do. Let's have a closer look at each of them.

The Patron–Client Economy

Society during my earthly indwelling functioned in a kind of multi-tiered system, with everybody competing to climb up the ladder of power and prestige. There were the patrons, who held monopolies over property and wealth, and there were the clients at the receiving end. But in between were the brokers, who themselves were clients of some higher patron while also negotiating on behalf of a particular group of clients.

Some people, of course, never made it up that ladder. They just remained stuck at the bottom, and they were the people I had a special concern for. But it rapidly changed from being a concern to being a privilege. I quickly realized that these so-called underdogs were the very ones who welcomed me and took all sorts of risks on behalf of my dream and my vision. And because I did not play the power games of the patrons and had no time at all for brokering, they obviously did not like me and eventually joined forces with the religious authorities to get rid of me.

What I found repellent about this whole arrangement was the lack of any kind of liberating love. Everything was conditional on having power and control over. There was no love, trust, care, or mutual empowering. The whole thing was—and of course continues to be—alien to my relational matrix.

You mean to say . . .

JEDAIAH: Sir, you sound like someone who is advocating communism.

JOSHUA: What do you mean by "communism"?

JEDAIAH: Where people have no individual rights and everybody is condemned to remain at the lowest common denominator.

JOSHUA: I am talking about the highest common denominator, namely, unconditional love, which is a fundamental right conferred on us by creation itself. Of course it is also a duty—we are called to confer it upon one another and upon every aspect of creation.

JEDAIAH: Utopian idealism is fine for a preacher like you. The rest of us have to live in the real world and survive there.

JOSHUA: And do you honestly think you are "surviving"?

JEDAIAH: Well, we are trying to, as best we can.

JOSHUA: So you spend most of your time struggling to survive in a creation where you are all meant to thrive.

JEDAIAH: That's impossible. The survival of the fittest is the name of the game, and neither you nor any other guru is going to change that.

JOSHUA: I agree; if you decide it can't be changed, then from the human point of view it can't be changed. But there is more to life and to creation than just us, humans. And that is the point I keep making over and over again: we need to step out of our narrow human world to see what it's all about.

JEDAIAH: It's hard enough staying in it, never mind having to step out of it.

JOSHUA: When you take the risk, Jedaiah, you'll begin to see that the outer and inner are one.

Purity Laws

Of all the regulations that prevailed in my earthly indwelling, the purity laws seemed to dominate the entire religion of the day. For a culture that believed that life came through blood, it was amazing how many taboos existed around anything to do with blood. Sex was the other great demon. In fact all body fluids were considered suspect, which of course reflected a huge phobia around the meaning of the body itself.

I never even bothered trying to observe those purity laws. My earthly family were disgusted with me over that and embarrassed almost to the point of totally disowning me. I didn't stand a chance of being able to observe those rules, so what was the point of even trying? And anyhow, how could I go along with so much of that necrophilic outlook when my mission was about the fullness of life arising from unconditional love?

You mean to say . . .

REBECCA (*in a panic*): Sir, Judy has touched the end of your robe, and she has had bleeding for the past twelve years.

JOSHUA: Calm down, Rebecca, it's okay. I know she has touched my garment, and that's fine!

REBECCA: What do you mean it's fine. She is unclean and has now made you unclean.

JOSHUA: She's a human being; I am not worried whether she is clean or unclean.

THEODORE: Sir, do you realize what you are saying in front of all these people. Have you any respect at all for your religion, and for the faith of these people? Why are you disturbing the people's faith, and why such slander and disrespect for our beloved nation?

JOSHUA: We are not talking here about faith; we are dealing with oppression.

JUDY: O my God, I am going to cause a big argument here. Will I ever get anything right in my life!

JOSHUA: Judy, you're okay. You are a normal, healthy woman, riddled with the weight of guilt and shame. Rise above your oppression and be whole once more.

THEODORE: What is he onto? And he has TOUCHED someone unclean, and worse still a WOMAN!

JOSHUA: Get to hell out of here and leave this woman alone.

Scarcely a day went by that I didn't run into some hassle over these laws of ritual purity. They seemed to dominate everything in the lives of those people and of course still haunt your understanding of sexuality. Your sexuality is the erotic energy of the divine itself, one of the most beautiful and volatile gifts of my relational matrix with which you have been endowed. So why have you demonized it in the name of this purity phobia that has haunted you for the past two thousand years?

The Patriarchal Family

I had a terrible time with my family. Talk about a dysfunctional system, but then it was not their fault. The culture of the day was riddled with control systems. Miriam, my mother, was a wonderful woman, but in the family system she was a nobody. All the power was invested in the dominant male. Children had no rights in my day, despite all the rhetoric about the family being essential for the love and nurturance of children. It was a system for disciplining children rather than for loving them.

I never wanted to be too closely identified with any earthly family, because my primary family is the relational matrix, and using the family as a power structure is a total antithesis of what the matrix is all about.

You mean to say . . .

VOICE 1: Sir, your mother and brothers are outside looking for you.

JOSHUA: Who are my mother and brothers and sisters? Those committed to my new dream, to the vision of the New Reign—those people are my mother and brothers and sisters.

VOICE 2: What is he onto now—has he any respect at all for his family?

VOICE 1: Sir, they have been looking for you for days and they urgently need to see you.

VOICE 2: They are wondering if you love them anymore or if you have abandoned them completely.

JOSHUA: In my relational matrix we love everybody, and primarily those who seek to establish unconditional love across the whole of creation.

VOICE 1: Would you please go and talk to your family and stop all the silly preaching for a while.

JOSHUA: We must first work at establishing the order of unconditional love and then every other relationship will fall into place.

VOICE 2: The man is out of his mind.

It was not easy to get it right with my people. They were all heavily involved in family life, and they thought that essential for right living here and hereafter. They meant well. My problem with them was the complicity with the prevailing power system. It was so alien to well-being—human and planetary alike—and in the long term it had nothing of value to offer. They lived in fear and in submission. I wanted them to know the liberating power of unconditional love. To get that across was a real struggle—and two thousand years later, it remains an awesome challenge!

Poetic Echoes . . .

Blessed is the patriarch who would never condescend.
Blessed is the master on whom slaves would not depend.
Blessed is the prodigal whose sin we can forgive
So that love could walk afresh upon our land.

Blessed is the disciple with little in the sack.
Blessed the persecuted who for justice took the flak,

Blessed are those who hate you and you do not hate them back,
So that love can walk afresh upon our land.

Blessed are the women and the birthing they proclaim.
Blessed at the margins are the sick and blind and maim.
Blessed is the leper who stigma overcame,
Because love can walk afresh upon our land.

Blessed is the Mother who could not figure out.
Blessed are the seekers at home in search and doubt.
Blessed are the dreamers who risk another way to mold.
So that love can walk afresh upon our land.

Blessed the one whose stretcher was lowered down through
*   the roof.*
Blessed is the woman who anointed him to soothe.
Blessed is the beggar at a gate he did not choose,
Because love can walk afresh upon our land.

Blessed the little children whose rights are guaranteed.
And blessed the liberators outwitting power and greed.
Forever, such blessings are graciously decreed.
For love has walked afresh upon our land.

EPISODE NINE

Did I Work Miracles?

THE PROBLEM WITH THE QUESTION of miracles is that you humans rarely start in the right place. You are so blinkered and deluded by this preoccupation with power and dominance that you always tend to miss the bigger picture. That more than anything else is your spiritual, cultural, and human crisis.

For me and my relational matrix, cosmic creation is the greatest miracle ever wrought. There is a kind of magic by which the whole thing works. I call it beauty, and I am delighted that at least a few scientists have recognized it as the clue to everything else. The only thing I'd say to the scientists is this: the beauty is not just in the mathematical formulae; the mathematics point to the beauty because the beauty is already there.

Creation and Fragility

What impresses my relational matrix about the cosmic beauty is the fragility upon which it survives and thrives. From the earliest moments of the material creation, matter and anti-matter dance an arcane minuet poised on the edge of extinction. Creation has been at this threshold billions of times since then, yet things never come to nought. Individual species come and go. Galaxies flare into existence and explode in smithereens, stars evolve over billions of years and explode as supernovae. Birth, death, and rebirth flourish at an astounding rate. That, my friends, that more than anything else, is the primordial miracle upon which every miracle is based.

Unless, and until, we appreciate the miracle of creation in its paradoxical grandeur of birthing and dying—forever to be reborn— we really can't understand any miracle, including those in the Christian Gospels. All miracles arise from a power for coherence and connection that characterizes my relational matrix and every relationship thereafter. The secret power of the miracle is not in some divine magic but in the unlimited potential of cosmic relational energy.

You mean to say . . .

ABRAM: Are you trying to tell us that you are not of God?

JOSHUA: I am trying to help people discover the divinity with which everything in creation is endowed including the human heart.

ABRAM: But that doesn't matter; leave all that to the philosophers. What I need to know is the truth, and I need proof of that truth by seeing miraculous signs performed.

JOSHUA: And after that, all will be fine?

ABRAM: Of course, 'twill be fine! I will then be able to distinguish truth from falsehood, the true God from all these false idols.

JOSHUA: In other words, Abram, you will then feel that you are in charge! And if you are in charge, then please tell me, how can God be in charge?

ABRAM: Why do you always get into these philosophical arguments? I want to see evidence for God and then I can believe.

JOSHUA: But the evidence is all around you and has been for billions of years. Open you eyes, man! And learn to trust . . .

Miracles happen when relationships are based on love, trust, and truth. People who seek miracles for sensationalism, power, or "proof" of divine existence are going to be disappointed. Miracles belong to the ordinary, not the extraordinary. Look into the eyes of an infant gurgling and cooing to its heart content, or the wrinkled face of an old woman in graceful resignation, or a squirrel playing in a spruce tree, a snow-capped peak of the Himalayas, a weary justice worker who has given everything to lift the plight of people with HIV/AIDS—there's your miracle as clear as you'll ever see one!

Miracle of Abundance

But let's get back to the three features I mentioned: love, trust, and truth. Take the story of the feeding of the multitudes. I had to work that one several times before people learned to live differently—and to share with trust. On one occasion a storm was brewing and several of the folks were a long way from home. Many just couldn't make up their minds whether they'd stay put or risk the journey home. One way or the other, they felt they had to cling tenaciously to the food they had, little or plenty. The more fretful they became, the less they would share even a morsel of what they had.

So I called over little Raphael, young, trusting, and generous in heart. I asked if he would share some of his pack-lunch with me, and he agreed. There we sat, munching away to our heart's content. So says I to the folks: "Come on folks, Raf and I are sharing our food, why don't you do the same; we'll all feel the better for it and will be better prepared for what lies ahead." Slowly but surely, love broke through, trust unfolded, and the truth became transparent. These people had plenty of food, but fear and greed were preventing them from sharing it.

Yes, indeed, they all ate and were filled. They called it a miracle—absolutely right! But it was a miracle of sharing, not of multiplying. The magic is not about some secret power of mine, but about the marvels that can happen when we allow love, trust, and truth to guide and govern our lives.

Healing Sickness

Searching for miraculous power or some type of divine magic has led believers and even scholars to some preposterously false conclusions. At the heart of many miracle stories is a very simple (but profound) readjustment of values and attitudes. This is even more true in the case of people afflicted with illnesses of body, mind, or spirit.

Your doctors and nurses, at heart, are good people, and they mean well. But they operate a health-care system that is quite convoluted and at the end of day brings neither healing not cure to millions of people. They look on the human body in a very mechanistic way, and they play all kinds of power games trying to control what is going on in peoples' lives. They are addicted to curing, but they know very little about healing and wholeness.

So many people to this day are sick because of guilt, oppression, systemic evil, exclusion. It is not the sick condition that needs to be rectified but the context that caused the condition in the first place. Oh dear, what arguments I had with the scribes and Pharisees on that one! They were so brainwashed with the notion of God punishing people for wrongdoing—and they love it because it reinforces their craving for control over people's lives. What a bizarre and barbaric understanding of the divine!

You mean to say . . .

BEN: You use all these magic tricks and then claim that it is the power of Adonai. Why are you trying to lead the people astray?

JOSHUA: What gives you the impression that the people are being led astray? Ask the people themselves if they feel they are being led astray.

> BEN: These people are common rabble; they don't understand the ways of God. We work hard to try to teach them and then you come along and undermine everything we try to do, like healing somebody on the Sabbath?
>
> JOSHUA: And tell me, if an ox or an ass fell into a pit on the Sabbath day, would you not pull it out?
>
> BEN: I am talking about SERIOUS matters. Your problem is that you don't seem to be able to distinguish between what is serious and what is trivial. In fact, you trivialize everything that is sacred to our religion.
>
> JOSHUA: I question everything that undermines basic human dignity, and I empower people into life and wholeness.
>
> BEN: And what has that got to do with our religion?
>
> JOSHUA: I came that people may have life and have it to the full. And the fullness of life that I offer is bigger than our religion; in fact, it is bigger than all the religions put together.
>
> BEN: People, this man is a fake; don't allow yourselves to be misled by him.

During my earthly existence people suffered retardation because of what was regarded as evil forces that had taken over their lives. A lot of that was the result of oppressive religiosity and political disempowering, and often it took time, effort, and prayer-filled concentration to set them free from the culturally inflicted traumas that people were forced to endure. What the Gospels call possession by evil spirits was simply the result of being a people crushed and beguiled by the political and social possession of a brutal foreign regime and a religious system that left people riddled with shame, guilt, and inferiority.

The human body has an uncanny sense of reflecting the powers at work in the social and political body. The reason should be obvious from what I have said to you thus far: because everything in creation is interconnected and interdependent, the small reality (e.g., the human body) will always mirror what is going on in the larger system. And herein lies the whole secret to what miracles are all about. Dysfunctionality, that is, a breakdown in the power for right relating, leads to powerlessness, sickness, trauma, so-called possession, excessive fear of annihilation, and meaningless death; but that same power for relating, invoked on the larger planetary and cosmic scales, provides the resources and the wherewithal for health, recovery, and wholeness of being.

Take, for instance, people who were deaf, blind, and maimed—some for almost a whole lifetime. It was not the external condition I healed but the deep internal pain, the abuse, the hurt, and the anguish that had eaten deep into the inner souls. That had to be healed before they could experience release from the external bondage within which they had been constrained for many years. Intervention at the level of consciousness—confronting and illuminating the destructive wisdom with the penetrating light of Holy Wisdom (an altered state of consciousness)—was the precondition for the healing liberation. Thus there could be set free a more wholesome spirit, a healthier mind, and a bodily space wherein pain and illness could be integrated at the service of life.

We Share a Power to Heal

I know you are still wondering if I used some magic tricks? What I did use were strategies that today would be described as altered states of consciousness. That gift and propensity were far more freely and creatively used during my earthly indwelling than it is today. You people have become so mechanistic and rational in your thinking that you are no longer capable of trusting the deeply intuitive wisdom that can beget healing and wholeness in so many situations. I often invoked that power in helping people to bring trauma and deep pain to a place of healing, and so did several other healers in my time.

Sometimes I added ritualizations, using water, clay, oil, light, and other elements from nature. In my day, several people did these kinds of things. There was nothing exclusively divine at work here. These are resources and giftedness with which my relational matrix has blessed every human being. The problem is that you people have forgotten what it really means to be human. You have forgotten and abandoned the miracle that is your own very selves.

Indeed, if I did at the present time what I did during my earthly indwelling, the learned and holy people would also describe me as a fake. They would dismiss me as a new age charlatan or a postmodern maverick. So much of my healing, then and now, is about the inner soul and not just the outer body. It is about inner transformation and not just outer intervention. It is about causes of illness rather than treating symptoms. And it is about invoking the healing qualities of the earth itself to enable humans to live healthily.

Once again, folks, let me repeat, there is nothing exclusively divine about all this. This is the power for right relating that my relational matrix has bestowed on everybody—if only people would become aware of their true selves and live accordingly. The lack of miracles in your world today is not due to a lack of faith. In fact, you have too much faith and most of it is of the wrong type; that is what prevents miracles from happening.

A more spiritually enlightened humanity would be aware of the miraculous that is all around us and within us. Then we would know in our hearts the miracle that we ourselves are and the potential—individually and collectively—to make the world a better place.

Don't pray to me for a miracle. Rather, pray for the eyes to perceive, the mind to intuit, and the heart to know the love that transforms everything in creation, begetting that fullness of life to which every organism is destined.

Poetic Echoes . . .

I always remember the night that I bled,
The stain on the bed clothes embarrassed.
I felt isolated, unclean, and ashamed,
I was basically a non-one, disowned and unnamed,
Impure in the eyes of the world.

But Rachel had twelve years unclean and unknown.
Even doctors were scared to come near her.
But caution she cast to the wind of a rush,
His garment she grabbed in a desperate touch,
And the rest is a miracle story.

Benja went wild in a frenzied attack;
They say he's possessed so for God's sake stand back.
And the healing voice called for calm and restraint,
Releasing the trap that had bound him in pain.
The long journey home is beginning.

Some live in fear of suffering and death.
Others as outcasts are blind, maim, or deaf.
Let's begin with forgiveness—the miracle drug
Setting free all before it—for sinner and thug,
And then the miraculous looks normal.

The people need healing, perturbed and estranged.
The matrix of life is disrupted and maimed.
It's not just the people, but systems as well,
Chaining up freedom and turning life into hell.
The miracle begets a new option.

EPISODE TEN

Casting Out Evil Spirits

THE CULTURE OF MY EARTHLY INDWELLING was characterized by many forms of oppression. The Romans ruled the land of Israel with a heavy hand; the Jewish authorities imposed several rules and regulations; and people lived under the shadow of primitive fears and irrational beliefs.

What your scholars today call *internalized oppression* was rampant in the culture of my time. People felt betrayed even by God—no wonder they were looking for a Messiah! And their narrow religiosity had disconnected them from the very sources of enduring hope and authentic liberation. In truth, they were a people in exile, and that state of estrangement went much further back than just their one-time expulsion from the land of Israel.

The Power of Spirit

They had a lurid fascination with evil spirits. They invoked spirit power to explain anything and everything that defied human comprehension. But it always had to do with aspects of life they perceived to be bad or dangerous. They had lost the capacity to see spirit power at work in the good things also, and this really was the root of the problem.

You see, for some millions of years the human species detected spirit power at work in every realm of creation, especially in the movements of air, wind, and water, in the fertility of the soil, in the rhythm of seasons and in the cycle of birth–death–rebirth. And in an unspoken way—long before language evolved—humans befriended the inherent paradox that is so central to every aspect of my relational matrix. Thus, for your ancient ancestors, the Spirit was benign and fierce, near and distant, tangible yet unreal, intimate yet awesome, birth giver and death dealer at the same time. And remarkably the ancient ancestors could hold and honor those paradoxes in a way that people of this time are largely unable to do.

The ancient peoples, precisely because they lived in a symbiotic relationship with the whole of creation, could befriend that paradoxical sense of holy Spirit and allow themselves to be embraced by it. That was the symbiotic relationship on which humans, in conjunction with all other life forms, thrived for several thousands of years. As I mentioned previously, you humans did not always get it right, but for most of the six million years you have spent on earth, you have done exceptionally well. Your problem today—the one that also caused so much confusion during my earthly indwelling—is that you are trapped in the destructive shadow of domination and control, and frankly that is the crux of the problem when it comes to the issue of evil spirits.

The problem around evil spirits can be traced back some ten thousand years to the wake of the agricultural revolution. The breakthrough of that time lay precisely in the cultural appropriation of the fertile earth, imbued with vitality by the living Spirit of my relational matrix. But from the moment you began to commodify the land and fragment it into sections over which you wrangled and fought, you progressively lost the living connection with the living earth. You began to rape the womb that nourished and sustained you. From then on, the man-made spirit of divide and conquer subverted the power of living spirit. And the distortion became progressively more bombastic.

Haunting Fear

People succumbed to a culture of fear, guilt, estrangement, and, worst of all, gross disconnection from the great story of their evolutionary unfolding. The reductionism became culturally suffocating, psychologically overwhelming, and spiritually paralyzing. By the time of my earthly indwelling, people were haunted by ghostlike fear. They understood every form of illness as revenge from the divine for some wrongdoing committed by oneself or by a member of one's family.

All vulnerability was seen as a curse and the prohibitions concerning ritual purity plunged people even further into alienation and estrangement. Internalized oppression drove many people to behave irrationally. People went mad, not because of what today you call mental illness but because of internalized oppression of body, mind, and spirit. And death, which for so long had been integrated into the cycle of birth–death–rebirth now came to be seen as the supreme evil; this often led to convoluted acting-out in burial places, tombs, and caves.

Finally, the oppression became introjected to such a degree that in people's imagination it became a living spirit, variously named as Satan, the Devil, Beelzebul, Prince of Demons. To bring people to healing and wholeness often meant that one had to espouse these bizarre beliefs precisely in order to undermine and displace them. In the healing rituals, I invoked so called spirits to leave people—often quite explicitly. Inevitably, I ended up being accused myself of being possessed and of casting out the evil spirits through some evil power. The whole thing got very messy at times:

You mean to say . . .

JACOB: Please, sir, Joshua; Sir, please . . . come and help my
brother, Rick. An evil spirit controls him; he froths at the

mouth, and screeches and runs amok among the tombs. Please, Joshua!

JOSHUA: Okay, okay! First, go and ask him to leave the burial ground and let the dead rest in peace.

JACOB: No, Sir; no, I can't. He has himself bound in chains in there. He is fierce; he is out of his mind.

JOSHUA: Okay, let me go and talk with him.

JACOB: For heavens' sake, Master, be careful; he is a pure lunatic.

JOSHUA: Don't panic, man; your fear is only making his fear worse.

(*Later*)

JOSHUA: Rick, my good friend, what is distressing you?

RICK: Get away from me, you divine bastard. I know who you are a messenger from God. GET AWAY FROM ME!

JOSHUA: I adjure you, living spirit, to leave this man.

RICK: Don't take another step; we are legion and we will eat you alive!

JOSHUA: Come out of this man I command you.

RICK (*loudly*): AH . . OUCH . . . My stomach!!!! YOU DIVINE BASTARD!

ONLOOKER 1: He's frothing from the mouth, and his face is turning blue. I think he has collapsed.

JOSHUA: Please don't panic; just give him a few minutes and he'll come round.

RICK: Oh, for fuck's sake, what's happening to me at all?

JOSHUA: You are okay; just let me hold your hand for a moment, and you will begin to feel better.

ONLOOKER 1: He has touched a man with an evil spirit; he has defiled our sacred laws; keep away from him.

ONLOOKER 2: You know something—he casts out evil spirits because he himself is possessed; for all we know, he might even be a prince of demons.

ONLOOKER 1: Oh my God, he gave him a kiss; isn't he a despicable character! Has he any respect at all for our faith and the holy rules?

ONLOOKER 2: Joshua, get away from that evil man, and please leave our territory. We don't want dangerous people like you around here.

JOSHUA: Would you guys ever stop judging and pontificating and get the hell out of here.

ONLOOKER 1: Sir, we know how to handle these predicaments—according to the regulations of our faith.

RICK: Well, then, why were you not able to help me; I came to you three times and spent what money I had, but got damn all in return.

ONLOOKER 2: It's by the power of Beelzebul that he cast out your spirits; they'll come back to haunt you seven times worse.

RICK: Well, let's wait and see . . .

Sickness of Psyche

Many of the illnesses in my time, named as possession by evil spirits, today can be identified as traumatic or psychotic fits. Then, and now, they have nothing to do with being possessed or taken over by evil spirits. Rather they are distortions of the living spirit that inhabits every organic creature. There are several contributing factors—all symptomatic of the dysfunctional relationship with creation and with my relational matrix. These factors include living with extreme stress resulting from poverty, warfare, social dislocation, blatant exploitation, and injustice; psychological imbalance caused by social exclusion, racism, sexism, competitiveness; spiritual misadventure (as in drug abuse) or psychic neglect in a culture where external achievement and projected self-image are grossly exaggerated; and occasionally irregularities of health based on biochemical or hormonal deficiencies. But again, let me emphasize, all these illnesses arise because of your dis-spirited way of living, estranged to a frightening degree from the enlivening Spirit that inebriates creation at every level, planetary and cosmic alike.

Therefore, let's not relegate the notion completely to the confused, oppressed culture of two thousand years ago. Contemporary cultures are also replete with Satan-like distortions. Many addictive behaviors of this time—whether related to alcohol, gambling, sex, the fascination with money, the compulsive attachment to power—take over lives with an overwhelming possessiveness. These addictive allurements, many sanctioned and enforced by the dominant culture of this time, are not easily broached, and frequently can only be resolved by embracing a spiritually informed resolution.

Systemic Evil

I am also very concerned about the evil monstrosities that ravage human and planetary life today, especially at a systemic level. Take money, for instance. Money is a form of electronic energy that flows around planet Earth with increasing rapidity and sophistication. Like all forms of energy, it is imbued with spirit power. It symbolizes and celebrates abundance, flourishing, affirmation, and achievement. As a form of energy it can be benign or malignant depending on how humans choose to use or abuse it. It is painfully obvious that it is not being used by you humans in an inspired, informed, and enlightened way.

Of course, the abuse of money is really an abuse of power. And as you will hear me say many times, I believe that the abuse of power is the most pernicious evil operative in the human world today. The living Spirit of my relational matrix liberates the capacity for flourishing at every level of creation, from the ancient stars to the tiny bacteria. The Spirit's desire to empower adorns every sphere and age of creation. But the freedom to empower has been seriously undermined by those people and structures that appropriate power unto themselves with little or no awareness of what power is intended for.

The ruling institutions epitomize the force of evil spirit in today's world. Whether managed by presidents, popes, prime ministers, economists, advertisers, or executive directors, they brutalize the power of the living Spirit, relegating it to their own commodified ends and correspondingly stripping creation and all its creatures of the capacity for growth and flourishing.

The forces of evil I encountered in my earthly indwelling were mild compared with the domesticated satanic forces of this age, camouflaged under the veneer of political, social, economic, and religious governance. Whenever creatures—human or otherwise—are disenfranchised in terms of their innate spiritual capacity for flourishing and mutual empowerment, the forces that disempower begin to feel like superior spirits. The disempowerment even undermines the ability to name reality truthfully; lies and falsehoods become the prevailing truths.

During my earthly indwelling, people felt baffled and overwhelmed by evil spirits. Tragically, little has changed on this front, except that the beastly icon is no longer something that infests the individual human soul. Rather it has infiltrated the major institutions and their modes of governance, driving a widespread systemic desire for raw power and a largely unexamined agenda committed to the philosophy of divide and conquer.

Prayer and Fasting

How do we expel these cultural and systemic demons? Well, a little prayer and fasting would certainly help! I mean prayer that will enable and empower people to discern more clearly and boldly the truth of what is going on around them, a truth that will illuminate the corruption and exploitation that are rife in the political and economic institutions of our time. Fasting as a discipline provides inner clarity, a restive spirit, enlightening our choices on where we should place our creative energy—at the service of those subversive movements that beget creative alternatives, and not at the service of exhausted imperial forces, which, for the greater part, are no longer capable of delivering inspirited life or enduring meaning.

Humans, you do have choices! And this is a time for prophetic choices, not for the respectable, conventional ones that no longer liberate enduring truth. You have chosen wisely for most of your time on earth, and although you now face momentous hurdles, the empowerment of my living Spirit is always with you to assist you at this precarious time. If you live by the Spirit, you will grow in meaning, dignity, and purpose. It you fail to adhere to the true Spirit, then assuredly you too will be haunted by forces that at times will feel overwhelming. You have the choice, and I hope you will choose wisely.

Poetic Echoes . . .

They came in their anguish, possession was rife,
Exorcists employed by the dozen.

They dealt with the symptoms and 'twasn't enough.
The Spirit still wallowed in bondage.

Disease in the soul and sickness of mind
and empowering Spirit corrupted.
They stood little chance to partake in the dance
that augured in freedom abundant.

To try and make sense of the torture inside
they began to project rather wildly.
And they frenzied with froth, in eyes, ears, and mouth
to release the raw pain that entrapped them.

It was not the sins of the fathers come back.
It was not some curse from the Godhead.
But internalized pain from imperial reign
had twisted and broken their spirits.

So, spirit re-membered I first did retrieve,
re-aligning the fractures of torture.
For Spirit is wholesome and binds into one
what is broken, and battered and damaged.

'Twas hard to believe for the witnessing eye.
The dreaded possession intrigued them.
And if I cast them out, they reasoned aloud,
I too was possessed by a demon!

But healing broke through and hope was invoked
and the Spirit restored liberation.
And empowering stories began to release
grace and freedom for wholesome relating.

EPISODE ELEVEN

In Memory of Her

THE PREACHERS IN THE CHRISTIAN churches like talking about discipleship, but unfortunately they often miss the point of what real discipleship is about, either now or in my earthly indwelling. I find it irritating how neatly they present the whole thing. If only they could realize how complicated and awkward it often was for me, and for those who felt the call to follow me.

Many of those people made enormous sacrifices and took big risks with their safety, their security, and their lives. And, of course, they followed me for a whole range of reasons. Only a mere handful got the whole picture. The vision of my relational matrix was beyond most of them. However, I will count my blessings and be grateful. They did try, and in my eyes that is what really matters.

The Twelve and More!

Your preachers often associate discipleship with the so-called twelve apostles. The story of the twelve has been blown out of all proportion. They are more an invention of the early Christian church than key players in my earthly indwelling. You see, the problems began when they considered me to be the long-expected Messiah. They traced all sorts of genealogies to establish that I belonged to a pure Jewish line and that I was the one to fulfill the prophesies of the Hebrew scriptures. And I ask myself, now as then, what has all that got to do with my relational matrix, which embraces the whole of creation and all nations and peoples within it.

Anyhow, in their concern with my Jewish origins and context, they became preoccupied with the tradition of the twelve tribes of Israel and so insisted that there had to be a group of twelve that they claimed should be more important for me than anybody else. Well, I am sorry, folks, but my relational matrix doesn't work that way.

We don't go in for that type of selectiveness; I find it exclusive and snobbish. I wanted variety and diversity in my followers, and so I called many different folks, just as I still do today. And the more unworthy they feel, the more I want them with me!

Now, this story is dragging on, and I still have not come to the main point. I want to tell you about one memorable woman who was an apostle, a disciple, and a great deal more. Her name was Mary of Magdala. What a woman! I'll never forget her. Of course, she was only one of several women who were among my close followers, who showed me incredible love and care and often made huge material and financial sacrifices for my itinerant community.

A Woman with Demons

Mary of Magdala first came to see me in a state of awful distress. She was a bright woman, with a searching, curious mind. She was highly intelligent, and her intelligence was nearly her downfall. She was intrigued and fascinated by Goddess traditions and felt that they had far more to offer women than the oppressive impositions of Judaism. She was a feminist far ahead of her time.

Her story was that she became so preoccupied with the Goddess and Goddess icons that they began to take over her life. That's how she explained it to me. And the head trip became more and more emotionally and spiritually confusing. In the end she convinced herself that she was demon-possessed; and, of course, everything in her culture was quick to endorse that misguided perception. She had terrible nightmares, hallucinations, and, it seems, blackouts. Not only was it causing havoc in her personal life, but it also became a painful affliction for all her loved ones.

She sought help from a number of reputable healers. She had some temporary relief, but each time something worse caught up with her. She sought refuge among the disciples of John the Baptist, and one of them sent her to me. To be honest with you, all she needed was a lot of basic human reassurance. The more some of these healers piled on prayers and rituals, the worse they made peoples fear evil spirits. And fear was the big issue that needed attention in the process of healing and bringing a person back to wholeness.

After a few sessions, she was relieved of her affliction and gradually began to restore her well-being. At that time, my itinerant community was beginning to take shape, and there was a wild sense of enthusiasm around. Many of those earlier followers sensed that we were onto something of significant importance. They had no idea what it was, and—to be perfectly honest with you—I was not too sure myself. That is what intrigued me about Mary of Magdala. She was so insightful, perceptive, and contemplative. Having her around was sheer joy, and the longer she wanted to stay, the happier I was to have her.

A Prophetic Outcast

Unfortunately, that caused problems I had not foreseen. She had been away from her home and family for several weeks. Although they had expected that in terms of her exorcism, they were assuming that the time would have been spent in prayer and penance rather than in the company of a new group associated with messianic expectations. Sadly, her family misread the whole thing. They already had heard of me, from those who not only did not like me but considered me a threat to their faith and their culture. When Mary informed them that I had rid her of the evil spirits, they jumped to the conclusion, quite common at the time, that I must be possessed and that consequently Mary was now in liaison with the prince of demons, and in their eyes totally beyond salvation.

It was a bizarre twist in what should have been such a wonderfully liberating story. Her family kicked her out—totally disowned her. Some months later, when I accompanied Mary to her home, we got a cold, hostile reception. I felt so upset and angry about the whole thing— another tragic example of what false religiosity does to people.

That is how Mary ended up being one of my followers. Both I and she had hoped that a reconciliation with her family would eventually happen, and I did everything I could to support that outcome. Unfortunately, it never happened—despite several encounters with members of her family over many years.

I always made it a priority to treat each of my followers as unique and special, and to exercise as much equality as possible in our inter-actions. But I must confess, it was difficult when it came to Mary of Magdala. Apart from being an extremely attractive woman, her capacity for leadership, initiative, insight, and morale were far in excess of my other followers. The fact that her own life had been through the crucible of pain, suffering, family rejection, and so much misunderstanding made her all the more authentic and reliable.

But it was her way with the other followers that left a lasting impression. When their spirits were down, when they were full of doubts and wondering what it was all about, her reassurance and ability to convey fresh hope were truly unique. She became a natural leader among the women disciples, and I am eternally grateful to her for the way she befriended my own mother. Indeed, if it hadn't been for Mary of Magdala, I would have been as much of a reject in my family as she was in hers.

It did not take long for her too to carve out a distinctive role among the male followers. Some of them resented this, and her one-time close friendship with Judas did not go down too well. But over time, they began to trust in her wisdom and seek her advice. She was a wonderful person to build relationships and nourish sustaining community among the followers. It puzzles me why it took two thousand years for the Christian churches to acknowledge her as the apostle to the apostles. It was so obvious!

Anointed for Mission

I have many cherished memories of Mary being there for me when I felt weary and out of sorts. Her attentive listening and empathetic presence often brought peace to my soul and reassurance that the mission was worth all the opposition and misunderstanding. And Mary had a wonderful gift for ritualizing distinctive moments of experience; sadly, few of them are recorded in the Gospels, but one of the most memorable is recorded. As I recall, the conversation on the occasion it went something like this:

> MARY: Joshua, I have anointed you before, and poured balm over your weary feet. But this is a special kind of anointing, the type I hope will strengthen you for the difficult times ahead.

JOSHUA: So, you share my opinion, Mary, that things are reaching a crucial stage.

MARY: You know, Joshua, I get these strong premonitions at times, even vivid dreams. I had one just a few nights ago. It is almost impossible to talk about, it feels so frightening.

JOSHUA: In Jerusalem, Mary?

MARY: Yes, Joshua, in Jerusalem.

JOSHUA: Well if that is where destiny is leading me, that is where I need to be.

MARY: How I wish we could do something to avert such a calamity, but in some inexplicable way, it feels like it is a price we all have to pay, and why you rather than just the rest of us, I just don't understand.

JOSHUA: Fear not Mary; my relational matrix will bring all things right. Meanwhile, let's have the anointing.

MARY: By the power of this holy anointing, may you know strength in your inner being; power from on high for this hour of anguish, and the grace to pour all your visionary grace into this precarious moment.

JOSHUA: Amen.

JUDAS: Hey, why did you waste all that expensive oil; that is worth at least three hundred denarii.

MARY: Don't worry, Judas, you'll understand someday.

JUDAS: I do understand, far better than a reckless emotional woman like you could ever hope to understand.

JOSHUA: Lay off, Judas, and leave her alone.

JUDAS: Master, you are too easily influenced by this woman. We know she is very wise, but she behaves in extreme ways at times. This oil could easily have been sold and the money given to the poor.

JOSHUA: Judas, you always have the poor with you, but you won't always have me.

JUDAS: What does that mean?

JOSHUA: She was anointing me for the precarious time that lies ahead, a truth she can comprehend, and few others can.

ONLOOKER (*to Judas*): By the way, Sir, does your Master realize that he has been touched by a woman who has a bad reputation in the town. Dangerous business this!

Mary knew how to defend herself against these kinds of attacks, yet she was a woman of measured words and certainly did not waste time on those with other agendas. She gathered whom she could among my followers and informed them that things looked ominous, and that, indeed, it would be something of a miracle if I came through the forthcoming Passover time unscathed. On this occasion, the men gave her little heed. Worse still, some of them blamed her for bringing about my final demise.

The rest is history: the tragic betrayal of my male followers; the incredible fidelity of the small band of female disciples, with Mary's unrelenting conviction holding them in solidarity to the bitter end. She did not falter in the face of the serrating pain and confusion that characterized my untimely death. And it was Mary's outrageous hope that gave birth to what your scholars now call resurrection.

This is a woman who stood head and shoulders above us all. She was a champion of my New Reign. She cherished memories and set new flames alight. Under her persistent and audacious inspiration, the primitive body of believers began to take shape. Fortunately she was around for long enough to see the fledgling church come into being. Ironically, she was progressively relegated into the background by the male folks who thought that they alone had access to divine truth.

But the real truth wins out in the end. It always does. And Mary of Magdala will not be forgotten. In fact, wherever the truth of my relational matrix flourishes, there her name will be held holy and her apostolic uniqueness will be proclaimed and celebrated!

Poetic Echoes . . .

Tortured body, troubled mind, ailing figure gaunt;
Driven to insanity by oppressive darkness.
I remember it all too well!
As, indeed, I do the moment I touch your
Reeling body curled up in fetal trepidation.

Mary, it was but your first taste of Calvary,
Your darkest hour of limitless despair.

But you broke through the anguish and the pain
And ever thereafter would call despair to task
Beyond all our empty tombs,
To the fearful, liberating paradox of Resurrection.

Mary, you enflamed our hearts with inspiration.
Discipleship infiltrated the recesses of your being.
You knew our questions and our doubts,
But you kept us on our toes,
For there's no going back when the furrow
Of the Kingdom is carved upon the sands of time.

It led you to Calvary and beyond
On a wet and forlorn Easter morning
Engulfed in blood-stained clouds,
You rolled away the stone of morbid doubt
And while the waiting world shivered on the edge of despair
Once more you held your nerve, to raise our dwindling hopes.

Befriend, today, our pilgrim hopes
When dreams are crushed by demonic forces,
When petrified disciples flee in fear,
When misogynist clerics try to steal the living soul.
Mary, you are the catalyst of Resurrection promise.
Patriarchy won't last forever.
It, too, will wield a cross on a Calvary hill,
And from its ashes the sphinx will rise,
And, no doubt, Mary, you will be there as you were of yore.

And this time they will recognize you
For the one you really are: Mary of Magdala!
First among all the Apostles
And from this day forward,
Pregnant echoes will reverberate:
Holy is your name!

EPISODE TWELVE

Salvation: What a Price!

You mean to say . . .

ROSEMARY: Tell me exactly, what does it mean when people say, "saved by the blood of Christ?"

JOSHUA: I wish I knew (*pause*). In the time of my earthly indwelling, people held the view that blood was a carrier of life energy. Today we would see it as one of several energy flows that make up a living organism. Life belongs to several elements of cosmic and planetary creation and not just to blood.

ROSEMARY: So shedding blood was considered to be about giving life?

JOSHUA: Yes, that would have been the idea.

ROSEMARY: I can understand that from a woman's point of view. We shed blood in order to give life. Shedding blood is very much part of our reproductive capacity, but this idea of men shedding blood—which is nearly always about violence—I don't see how that could be salvific or redemptive.

JOSHUA: Good for you, Rosemary, I totally agree. This is one of the biggest blunders ever made in the name of religion.

DAMIEN: But isn't it clearly stated in our holy scriptures that the lamb is slaughtered for the salvation of all, that sacrifice has to be made to make up to God for the sins of humanity?

ROSEMARY: But who said that—the scriptures, or those who wrote the scriptures?

DAMIEN: But the scriptures are the inspired word of God.

ROSEMARY: Maybe they are inspired for men, but they are not very inspiring for us women. Anyhow, my question to you, Joshua, is: How do you understand your death, and all they have said about it being the source of our salvation?

JOSHUA: That's a complicated one. Where shall I begin?

T HOSE LAST DAYS of my earth-bound indwelling—indeed, I remember them well. I knew in my heart that the writing was on the wall, but at that stage I also knew there was no going back. The dream had to be honored and in the paradoxical situation in which I found myself, a price had to be paid.

There are three things that happened that last week, and what the Christian faith has done with those three events, to be honest with you, I think it is outrageous. In fact despicable!

As you know, I love food, and definitely for me the outstanding memories of my earthly indwelling are the meals I shared with friend and foe alike. If people could only honor my tradition of meal sharing, we could rid the world of want and starvation in a matter of decades. But, you see, it is difficult to know what I was about when you get off on a wrong start. I am referring to what Christians call the Last Supper.

A Special Supper

Actually it was not my last meal, although close enough to it. As I have already said, I had a strong hunch that the game was up. I posed such a threat to the autocrats, I knew they were desperately searching for a way to get rid of me and when the opportune moment would arrive, I knew it would be all over in a matter of hours. And hours it was, not days!

My female followers, Mary of Magdala, Rebecca, Joanna, and the others—they, too, were reading between the lines and did everything they could to protect me. Wonderful women, so perceptive and insightful, loyal and faithful; yet the Christian Gospels scarcely acknowledge their existence.

One day I suggested to the women that we should gather and have a kind of special meal, look back on what had been achieved and look ahead to what would have to be embraced. All the women turned up for that meal and a number of men also, and as for the twelve—well, they were conspicuous by their absence. In fact, I can't recall any of them being there. You see, once they got whiff of a possible execution, they fled as fast and as far as they could, in case they, too, would suffer the same fate. Talk about a petrified group of people. Time and again I tried to reassure them.

You mean to say . . .

JOSHUA: Friends, I don't understand it fully myself, but I know a day will come when the authorities will capture me and put me to death. I am afraid it's the price that has to be paid.

APOSTLE: What the hell is he onto now! You know, Master, you scare the living daylights out of me at times—and it's not good for my blood pressure!

JOSHUA: Have no fear; there is meaning and purpose to this although I can't fully explain it to you.

APOSTLE: We're not worried about purpose or meaning. The question is, How can we protect you? Hey, guys, let's go and purchase a few swords!

JOSHUA: Those who live by the sword will die by the sword. This is a destiny to be endured, not a battle to be fought.

APOSTLE: Endured for what? We have left everything to follow you. And now you're telling us the whole thing might come to nothing.

JOSHUA: I didn't say it would come to nothing. I said it might mean crucifixion and death, but that will not be the end. A rising to new life will follow, and I want you to be there to experience it.

APOSTLE: Fat lot of use that will be to us, with our jobs gone, and we're left with no one to lead us.

JOSHUA: Do not be afraid; I will be close to you always just as my relational matrix holds all creation in loving embrace.

APOSTLE: Okay, that's enough of that depressing talk. Let's go fishing for awhile!

Now, regarding this event called the Last Supper. There were a number of people there comparing it to a Passover meal of the Jewish faith and genuinely trying to reassure and console me for what lay ahead. But to be honest with you, I had no intention of becoming a lamb sacrificed for the salvation of the world. I just wanted to celebrate with friends who meant so much to me in life, and as far as I was concerned that meal was all about *life* and not about *death*. As for pronouncing special words, I said nothing at that meal that I hadn't already said several times at the other meals I shared with my friends.

Why do Christians isolate that last meal of mine and give it such a distorted significance? What I find particularly repulsive is the way it is used to justify an exclusively male priesthood. That really is an abomination and a tragic interpretation of the whole event. Basically that last meal belongs to the meal-sharing tradition that is so central to my vision of the New Reign, and it is about time you Christians stopped isolating it from its true context and distorting it to bolster the seditious ambitions of ecclesiastical power.

A Ritual of Washing

Next, I want to talk about the washing of the feet. I often did that for my followers just as they often did it for me, and that was how I learned how wonderful and meaningful it was as an experience. In Judea of my time, the roads were all dirt tracks, covered in dust and grit. And most people walked. There was a custom that when you invited a special guest for a meal—and, sadly, in the patriarchal culture of my day that always meant a male guest—the first thing you did was provide a bowl of clean water and some oils in which you bathed the feet of the special guest. It was a ritual of welcome and a very important one in my culture.

Regarding me as a special guest, my followers, both male and female, often bestowed the favor upon me. But I did not like the male exclusiveness of the whole thing, because, for me, everybody at meals was special, particularly the "non-persons," those excluded by the brutality and oppression of my culture. I suggested to my followers that we transform this special custom from something distinctly exclusive to something that would make everybody feel welcome and included. The women loved it and so did the tax collectors.

But as for the twelve, so scared to let go of their insecurities, for them it was a step too far, and they made no secret of their disapproval. One evening, as we were about to gather for supper, I suggested to Peter that I would wash his feet. Well, let me tell you I didn't suggest it a second time. He got into one of his fulminations, and it was just impossible to get through to him.

You mean to say . . .

PETER: Joshua, have you any respect at all left for yourself and the authority you represent. People who wash feet are slaves, and nobody else should dream of doing it.

JOSHUA: But, Peter, we're all called to be slaves, in the sense that we are called to be at the service of everybody in the name of love and justice.

PETER: No way, Master, we are at the service of those in legitimate authority, and others should serve us when we exercise authority over them, and washing feet is for people with authority and not these diabolical ideas you are suggesting.

JOSHUA: In the vision of my New Reign, one of the ground rules is that you call no one on earth a parent-figure, because we are all brothers and sisters at the service of the relational matrix.

PETER: I wish you would stop talking about that relational matrix and talk the plain simple language of daily life where some people are in charge and others are not.

JOSHUA: Peter, why are you so preoccupied with the need for power? It has nothing to do with the real meaning of life. The power that really matters is the power of unconditional love, and it sounds, Peter, like you really need to let that enter your heart!

Poor old Peter, if he could only love himself a little, then the rest of us would have some hope of showing him the liberating power of love! Anyhow, the point I am coming to is this. The washing of feet has nothing to do with washing in the literal sense. It is all about welcoming, and from my perspective welcoming in a special way the oppressed, the marginalized, and the excluded.

Consequently, I shiver in horror at what you Christians do with this ritual. It is not about repeating a piece of external behavior— surely you have more imagination than that! But what bugs me altogether is the exclusive choice of twelve men whose feet are already scrubbed clean. What is all this sanitizing about; dirt and dust are also divine creations.

And why do you exclude the women? Women washed my feet far more often than men ever did. But worst of all, why repeat a piece of behavior for the sake of repeating it? That strikes me as downright stupid, a kind of morbid ritualism, desecrating a challenging and wonderfully inspiring ritual.

This is meant to be a ritual of welcoming, not a literalization of foot washing. Surely the significance of this ritual for your context is that of welcoming into your homes those who have no homes, sharing your table and hospitality with those who have nothing, breaking down boundaries of exclusion in order to stretch the horizons of inclusiveness.

I really thought it should be obvious what the ritual meant—then and now! Bad enough for Peter to miss the point, but for people to be still missing it two thousand years later just goes to show what religion can do to people's creative imaginations.

A Final Journey

So the end was approaching, I knew it in my bones. And deep in my heart I knew it was the beginning of the end for the old dispensation. So I set myself two targets: Jerusalem and the temple. It was important that my death should be seen not just as an individual event but rather as the death of the religious system itself. The time had come to demolish the sacred cows, thus liberating people to worship in spirit and truth. I headed for Jerusalem!

I was both unsure and unclear what the best strategy might be, and I was so bloody nervous I couldn't think clearly. Some of my followers were suggesting that I should ride triumphantly into the Holy City. Not again! Why do they persist in that crap of trying to make me a king! How many times do people have to be told that they are missing the point completely. I guess that is what happens to people when they are indoctrinated by the addiction to power, status, and privilege.

Okay, I said to myself: no point in trying the rational, logical approach here, so let's go for the symbolic. It is much more provocative and subversive. Okay, then, damn you all, I am a king! Let's go for it!

You mean to say . . .

PETER: Hurrah! Jesus is our king, our liberator, the Messiah from on high! Alleluia.

JOSHUA: Peter, no need to get so bloody hysterical.

PETER: Master, I have waited so long for this day, the fulfilling of the prophets and the glory of our people Israel. Alleluia, he is king!

JOSHUA: Hey, John and Simon, go to the small farm at the eastern outskirts, just off Orchard St. and tell the farmer that Joshua wants a loan of a donkey; we'll return it as soon as we are finished.

THOMAS: What do want the donkey for?

JOSHUA: For the kingly procession.

JOHN: But, Joshua, kings always ride on horses.

JOSHUA: Yes, I know . . . but I want to ride on a donkey, so please go and fetch one.

THOMAS: This is ridiculous. Hey, Peter, he says he wants to ride on a donkey. When did you ever hear of a king riding on a donkey?

PETER: Hey, Master, don't be so goddamned stupid. This is your hour of glory, man. Our people have been waiting for this for ages, the liberation promised from on high!

JOSHUA: Peter, get out of my way, and stop perpetuating this man-made dominance and control. I have asked for a donkey and I am getting a donkey.

PETER: Isn't this outrageous! The one time when we can really prove to the people that this is the divine Savior, our Messiah, and he destroys the opportunity once again. I don't know if I can continue following this guy anymore. He is such a letdown when it comes to the crunch!

Peter, goes through these phases. He is so needy in himself he just can't let go of the power and pomposity. I know he was bitterly disappointed when I chose to ride on a donkey, but I have to honor what I am sent to be about, and maybe in time Peter will begin to get the message. Yes, a donkey it had to be, and there was no compromising on the matter!

Kings always rode on horses, but I and my people, we loved the simple little donkey. Thomas and a few of the more learned guys were a bit baffled, recalling that the only time in the Jewish scriptures when a king rode on a donkey was when he was going to sign a treaty, conceding defeat. Those guys found it so hard to get the message of the suffering servant, the very thing that was giving me hope and meaning.

So there I am on the donkey, heading for the Holy City. They were waving flags and garlands, and some of them strewing their garments on the road—and I riding on the donkey, who had enough to do to transport me without all that paraphernalia. When they threw those palm branches in front of us you'd think they were trying to organize an obstacle race. The whole thing was a bit of a farce, but it was a good laugh, and if one is facing the gibbet, one may just as well laugh as cry!

Into the city we headed with bemused women and children looking out over half doors and various characters joining our procession as it made its way. The military were none too comfortable while the fellahs with tassels and phylacteries were rushing all over the place like mindless robots!

The atmosphere was tense, and it was as obvious as daylight that the scribes and Pharisees were infuriated. Subtle though the message was, they got it—a king riding on a donkey, the ultimate insult to the imperial system. The king is dethroned forever—the royal power is dissolved into the ordinary people as they go about each day riding their donkeys. It was one of the most innovative brainwaves I ever had. Truthfully, it is the most brilliant of all the parable stories, although your scholars never describe it as a parable.

The End . . .

Despite various attempts to halt me and the donkey, I got right into the precincts of the temple. I couldn't stomach the sham any longer, so I let my anger loose and put the tables and money flying in all directions. Straight to their faces, I confronted the extortionists about their racketeering and exploitation. Within minutes I was surrounded. You'd think I had brought a whole army with me for my self-defense—half the Roman Empire seemed to be out to arrest me. It took only a few soldiers, because I did not resist.

Obviously, they had their instructions. Passover was always a tense time in Jerusalem. So the orders clearly were: get rid of him as quickly as you possibly can. Within one hour they had me on the gibbet. No judge, trial, or jury—I don't know where the Gospel writers got all the stories about Herod and Pilate and the various juries trying to pass judgment on me and my behavior. That's the kind of thing that might have happened for people of reputation—I mean good reputation, the kind that goes with power and status. As for me, they saw me as a common criminal, a pain in the neck to the authorities who were determined to get rid of me as quickly as possible.

It wasn't that they crucified me; they actually butchered me, and I was dead within a few hours. Then they dumped my body in one of those common pits, and I hope the wild animals enjoyed the feast that followed. IT WAS ALL OVER—at least from the human point of view.

Poetic Echoes . . .

I think I was too young to die at the age of thirty-three.
And I've never been too keen on martyrdom.
Nor am I that much impressed with slaughtering paschal lambs,
Spilling blood to rescue and redeem.

The price we pay for living is in the life itself,
Resilient and creative all the way.
The more we have to offer, the more we do receive
In a universe prodigious to the core.

The people of my culture struggled long and hard and sore,
Crushed by an oppression from the top.

Their politics and religion were bombastic and bizarre,
Depriving them of wisdom and true hope.

The matrix of creation with relating at its core
These folks scarcely knew what all that meant.
Oppression kept them ignorant, with truth in short supply
I knew I faced a rather daunting task.

My focus was their living, to uplift their daily lot.
I modeled them a freedom that provoked.
The outcasts and the sinners were the first to come along,
While the rulers felt their privilege being choked.

'Twas the liberation praxis that scared the powers that be
Releasing new empowerment for the mass.
They did what they had done for much of history,
Seek a scapegoat to resolve the growing impasse.

They got me at the paschal time when I was at my best,
Releasing life for justice and new hope.
They killed me and they dumped me as a criminal aghast,
A fast and furious ending was my lot.

But dreams have a potential to outlive a guru's life,
And hope's reborn when failure seems to loom.
New life had been implanted in searching seeking hearts.
'Twould blossom in the Spirit's pregnant home.

EPISODE THIRTEEN

When Hope Defies!

H OW I WISH YOU humans, and all the religions invested in my
name, would honor the real ending. All that glamorizing about
trials before this one and that one, and all that tedious rhetoric
about sacrifice, salvation, redemption, and the power of the cross,

to be frank with you it is a load of nonsense and has done little to bring about a better world for any aspect of creation.

My death was quick, brutal, and without dignity. Personally, I'd prefer to forget about it. The real meaning of my story is in my life, not my death. Because my life was so provocative and threatening, the system could not tolerate me any longer. They tried to cut the whole thing short, but it was too late. The die was cast; the New Reign had been launched; the seeds were already sprouting. The fruit of my life—rather than my death—was going to survive. And survive it did!

The Faithful Few

For a while, it was touch and go. The survival of my story hung in the balance. Even many of those who followed me rejoicing became disenchanted and disillusioned. As for the twelve—I probably don't need to tell you—they all fled. Basically they were good people, but quite a letdown when the going got tough. So who remained: THE WOMEN! My good old friends, the women stood by me to the end! One day I hope history will exonerate them and thank them for what they did, not merely for me, but for all humanity!

The women gathered together and went searching for my body. They thought they might find bones and human remains in caves or crevices, but every place was empty. Quickly, they realized that there was no point living in the past—seeking the living among the dead! Deep in their hearts they knew that the future was guaranteed, so now they had to go forth and embrace it.

The powers that be had got rid of me—and even of my body. But my extermination opened new doors to my relational matrix, and where my earthly indwelling ended, my enduring Spirit now took over. The women recognized all that within a matter of hours—Oh, how I wish men would try to cultivate the power of feminine intuition!

Yes, I was gone—gone forever. They didn't even succeed in salvaging my bones, never mind my body. Yet they knew I was alive, really alive, in fact, alive in a way far more real than an earthly existence. And the women knew it—deep, deep in their hearts, the power of my living Spirit was for them as vivid and transparent as daylight.

After some weeks the twelve and several others came out of hiding: scared, curious, and incapable of comprehending as usual.

You mean to say . . .

WOMAN: So where have you been? You know Joshua was depending on you to be there with him when the going got tough, and you ran away!

APOSTLE: We didn't run away. We were just using common sense. We have wives and children to look after.

WOMAN: But you were invited to risk everything.

APOSTLE: And we would have risked everything if he had fulfilled our expectations as the Son of God, and not some new age freak—riding on a stupid donkey! We should have spotted the contradictions before.

WOMAN: So what were you expecting, some kind of a magical guru?

APOSTLE: We were expecting him to be the one who would set Israel free, the Messiah promised by our religion, with the might and power of our great God that he was supposed to be representing.

WOMAN: You can't have external freedom until you have internal freedom first. He was about liberating our hearts, to dream and think in a new way. That is the vision he has left us, and that is the vision we must now start working on.

APOSTLE: Start working on! Forget the whole bloody thing. It's over and done with. He is dead, so forget about him.

WOMAN: Well, sorry to disappoint you, guys, but he is not dead. He is no longer around in his bodily presence, but his vibrant Spirit is all over the place.

APOSTLE: What a load of nonsense! Hysterical women, always acting on their emotions!

WOMAN: Don't worry, mate, there is more to us than just feelings. There is intuition and imagination and that is what you all need if you want to experience this moment of resurrection!

APOSTLE: Resurrection? What do you mean by resurrection?

WOMAN: Why ask us? You yourselves heard Joshua talk about resurrection—rising to new life.

APOSTLE: We heard him say many things, but after all we have been through these recent weeks, the quicker we can forget about him the better.

WOMAN: We can't explain it fully, but we are of one mind and heart that he is present among us in a way far more real than we previously knew.

APOSTLE: He is alive among us? Unless I see in his hands the holes of the nails and put my hand in there and see the wound of a spear in his side, I will not believe.

WOMAN: Don't worry, you'll get there eventually. You were always a bit slow on the uptake, but I guess it will catch up with you when the time is right.

APOSTLE: Such bloody arrogance; some of these women think they know everything.

They thought the women were talking nonsense—they never gave the women much credit anyhow. But the women knew what they were talking about and, even in the face of massive skepticism, held on to the dream: the New Reign of my relational matrix.

Rising to New Life

That I was risen from the dead became the new myth. Fascinating, intriguing, and quite bombastic at times. For me and my relational matrix there is no distinction between the realm of the dead and that of the living. Creation is one unbroken continuum: the dead and the living share the same living space, but at different vibrational levels.

The realm of the dead is not some distant sphere to which one escapes, or from which one is "risen." My relational matrix inhabits both, and so does every living creature in potential form. My resurrected state is supposed to be one in which I am more real than I was in my earthly indwelling. It is more enduring, yes, but not more real. It could not be more real than my relational matrix, from which all relationality emanates, and relationality is the basis of everything in creation including what you Christians call "resurrection."

Again, Christians have this strange preoccupation with trying to prove my divinity, and I guess they consider resurrection a necessary prerequisite to substantiate that "proof." I find the whole thing a bit repugnant; it does not even make for good fiction and has proved to be a massive distraction from the things that really matter. You humans have not even come to terms with my humanity, so how could you make sense of my divinity!

Anyhow, as I said previously, I am not worried about my divinity, and I see no reason why you should be either. If you took my humanity seriously, you wouldn't have any problem with understanding my divinity, and you would quickly come to realize that resurrection is about a fuller flowering of my humanity at the service of the New Reign, rather than anything to do with proof of my divinity.

The problem with you humans is that you don't stay grounded, close to the earth, your primordial womb, close to creation, the primary revelation of my relational matrix. You waste so much precious time and energy fleeing into the realms of "divine" fantasy, trying to transcend to the heavenly realm in some nonexistent outer sphere. Stop deluding yourselves. There is one creation, one universe, the unfolding tapestry of my relational matrix. That is your true home, in life, in death, and beyond death. Creation itself is forever undergoing the process of resurrection-transformation. I had to undergo it, and so do you. Resurrection is not just about me; it is about all of us and also about the whole of creation, planetary and cosmic alike.

Now that is something else the scripture scholars did not get right. They developed these so-called resurrection appearances. Good stories, I agree, but rather misleading. From the Christian point of view, resurrection is not so much about me as about my followers. Resurrection is the hope that defies all hopelessness. It is the power from within that kept my followers faithful to the dream after the authorities got rid of me. Resurrection is that intuitive conviction that the dream of my relational matrix has not been subverted by my individual death and that, paradoxically, it is even more resilient because of it.

That's how the women understood it. Resurrection is not so much about me as about that relentless hope that awoke in the women's hearts and sustained them in the face of bewildering odds. Eventually, many years later, the twelve also came to know this hope, but they would never have reached that stage were it not for my women followers.

Honoring the Vision

And that, of course is the great tragedy of the past two thousand years. The early Christian church, blinkered in its allegiance to the prevailing power system, overidentified with dominant males and subverted the feminine vision. Now, after some two thousand years, the truth is haunting our landscape and, we hope, will evolve into a new dawn for all those crushed by the oppression of imperialism.

For you humans, two thousand years seems such a long time, and particularly when you tend to judge most things in terms of that time span. For me and my relational matrix, it is a mere second. We work with the big scale of all creation. We like things big, because the bigger the context, the more meaning will unfold. Reductionism is a killer! So don't worry if you have mucked up the Christian story for almost two thousand years; we'll forgive you for that! The big question is: Will you forgive yourselves?

So, friends, we need to outgrow the old-time religion. It had its day, and I know it still means a lot to the poor and oppressed of the earth. Devotional prayers and rituals do help people to survive hardship and oppression, but they do little or nothing to liberate people for that fullness of life which my relational matrix desires for all creatures. Beyond your churches, devotions, and rituals is the reality of creation itself. This is the primary abode of my relational matrix. It is also the relational web from which all of you draw life, vitality, creativity, and hope.

You humans have done some horrendous damage to the web of life—reckless, crude, and outrageous! But we'll forgive you. However, you had better make some drastic changes in how you live and relate with the web. Because if you don't, the wise and holy creation itself will take action, perhaps drastic action in the face of which your extinction may be the price that will have to be paid to set things right in the web of life.

It is not my desire, nor that of my relational matrix, that this should happen to you, but we designed you as creatures endowed with the gifts of freedom and choice. Because of our commitment to loving unconditionally, we never withdraw our gifts, but if you choose to abuse them consistently, you'll end up punishing yourselves. I do appeal to you to try to wake up and realize the disastrous course you have set for yourselves and the consequences that are sure to ensue if you don't drastically change your ways.

Please join me tomorrow in Kisangani. I will be joining the protest march against the Western Minerals Federation, mining the local resources not to give them back to the people of the Congo but to use them for their own wealth and power. That kind of exploitation hasn't much to do with resurrection or new life!

Poetic Echoes . . .

Now where the hell were they when I needed them the most,
The ones that all the churches do revere.
They were not there on Calvary, nor elsewhere to be seen.
Only women were around to offer hope.

Bewildered, scared, and broken, the women were confused,
Yet, faithfully they kept the light aflame.
They tried to do me honors, my body to embalm.
Even that much was snatched without reprieve.

Common sense alone would tell them how hopeless it all felt,
But women don't give up too easily.
And they knew you don't find living in the realm of the dead.
Now they would bring to birth true liberty.

Discerning through the scriptures, they recalled the echoed words
Of dying, indeed, but rising then once more.
And the aliveness of the dead one made sense within their souls.
And Easter was declared forever more.

They were women with a mission and, of course, had
*   always been.*
Discipleship had never been so clear.

The Reign of God had seeped into the fibres of their being.
The aliveness of their God was ultra real.

They met the male apostles, depleted and forlorn.
"He's risen, and we know it in our hearts."
But they ridiculed the women as they often did before.
They could not face the truth eternally.

I want to thank those women for fidelity and truth.
More importantly for wisdom so unique.
One day they will be honored when the truth breaks through
*   the mist,*
And the light of hope will shine for all to reach.

EPISODE FOURTEEN

Birthing Embodied Love!

THUS FAR, you have the story of my earthly indwelling. And I have told you something about my relational matrix, the springboard from which everything comes forth. My relational matrix is forever bringing forth new life and possibility. To do so is our essential nature, and it could not be otherwise. We forever give birth and rejoice with all creation in the emergence of new life and creative possibilities.

At this juncture I want to speak to you about time, and return to the topic of incarnation, which we explored briefly at the beginning of the story. I and my relational matrix are much more at home in timelessness rather than in time. We don't count time in terms of hours, days, or years. For us, there is no before or after; we live with a sense of an eternal now.

Some of your scholars claim that there is only the now, and so we should strive to live in the present moment. It seems to me that every now is molded from what emerges out of the past, and in turn takes shape and direction under the lure of an open-ended future. Past, present, and future are human categories of a time continuum that is bigger and richer than any single past, present, or future.

For me and my relational matrix, we encourage a particular vigilance concerning the future. That is the dimension that remains and always will remain radically open. Even my relational matrix can't predict what the future will bring, because if we had that foreknowledge, we would have robbed the future of its capacity for surprise, innovation, possibility, and adventure. And for me and my relational matrix these are crucial qualities of that fullness of life that we are forever birthing forth.

For my relational matrix, therefore, the now is each sacred moment made transparent by the lure of the open-ended future as we seek to make all things new. For many of you people, I know that sounds confusing and risky. Ironically, it becomes a bit easier to grasp if you could read the past with a bit more vision and imagination.

You humans don't handle the past very well. You cling to the past, often institutionalizing things that were never intended to last, solemnizing customs that were culturally conditioned from the beginning and dogmatizing truths that can only retain meaning when they are reinterpreted in each new era. You put a lot of emphasis on preserving tradition, which frankly is the surest way to destroy a tradition. When you try to preserve something living, you always run the risk of ossifying it, casting it in concrete and effectively immobilizing it to the point of extinction. Traditions need to be rethought, interpreted afresh, and reappropriated in a new way for the context of each new era.

Incarnation

Now let me talk to you about *incarnation* and use this notion to illustrate what I have said about time and timelessness. Your scholars tend to apply this word exclusively to me in my earthly indwelling. Another tragic example of stultifying reductionism! Incarnation literally means *coming in the flesh,* but metaphorically it denotes the affirmation of embodied existence in every shape and form.

Everything in creation, not just you humans, is endowed with a body. In all cases body is the medium through which the creative Spirit flourishes. Bodies are the dimension through which the birthing and rebirthing of creation happens. So, first, incarnation is about the energy of my relational matrix birthing forth all forms of embodied existence, including the cosmic and planetary spheres. Second, it is about the creative potential—dare I say, the erotic energy—in which all bodies interact to enrich my relational matrix. Yes, indeed, there is a sense in which I and my relational matrix are dependent on creation for our growth and development.

Creation is a kind of seamless web, thriving on the power of relationality, the heart of which is my relational matrix. Every connection that is forged throughout the cosmic process enhances the relational capacity of the matrix. A new delight is evoked; a new possibility released, a new dimension added to the ceaseless dance of existence. The struggle to connect meaningfully is also our struggle. Intimately, we know the pain, the anguish, the heartbreak, the joy of breakthrough, and the hope of better things to come.

When you weep, we weep. When a tree is felled prematurely, an animal in pain because of crazy experimentation, a teenager rebelling against authority, a couple at the their wit's end trying to make a relationship work, an African woman burying the last of her seven children because of AIDS, a Peruvian farmer seeing his last piece of land swiped by a transnational corporation, we, too, feel the pain, the helplessness, the rage, the cruel injustice.

You mean to say . . .

CYNTHIA: So why don't you do something! Why do you stand idly by! If you could create the mighty heavens and everything around us, why can't you make some intervention to change the plight of our awful suffering.

JOSHUA: Cynthia, if we tried to change it, people would jeopardize our attempt, as they have jeopardized so much more of what we have already been doing to empower humans.

CYNTHIA: Are you trying to say that we actually have power over you?

JOSHUA: In a sense, yes!

CYNTHIA: But that's ridiculous. If you can't change things, what hope is there for the rest of us.

JOSHUA: The hope rests not in what I and the relational matrix can achieve, but in what already has been achieved through the empowering we have been doing for billions of years.

CYNTHIA: It doesn't seem to have got you very far.

JOSHUA: I beg to differ, Cynthia; it has got us a great distance. Nearly everything we set out to achieve has been achieved. And even with you humans, things worked pretty well until you got stuck in this collusion with power about eight thousand years ago.

CYNTHIA: So what are we to do then?

JOSHUA: Learn to love and trust once more, just as you are unconditionally loved!

CYNTHIA: **W**e know all that, but HOW?

JOSHUA: Now, Cynthia, you are beginning to play a codependent game. You are expecting me to play the guru and provide all the answers to every predicament. Cynthia, you are an ADULT, in an ADULT world, endowed with all the giftedness adults need to live meaningfully. Perhaps, that is the first "how" you and your people need to face: to grow up and start behaving like responsible adults.

In fact, one of the crucial issues about incarnation is the amount of emphasis you humans put on the divine coming into the world as a little child. I love children, and I agree they are very special. But you need to be careful of how patriarchal culture manipulates the symbol of the child to make everybody else behave in childish subservience. My incarnation is primarily about being an adult, not about being a child, and that is a dimension Christians have scarcely started to come to terms with.

Now let's relate that to the time factor and you'll see what I am getting at. Your scholars seem to suggest that the incarnation of the divine in human existence (embodiment), happened for the first time about two thousand years ago. Where in the name of all that's good and holy did people get that bizarre notion? It is so narrow and reductionistic, and alien to the meaning of embodied existence. It is so time-constraining and grossly misleading, creating an appalling ignorance—and a childish codependence—not just about me (and the relational matrix) but about your own very existence as a human species.

Human Emergence

Once more, let's look at a few basic facts and try and honor them for what they are. You humans, as a human species, have been on this earth for over six million years. Many of you don't seem to be even aware of that, and all this emphasis on the two thousand years of Christendom has badly distorted your self-understanding. What's worse, it has left you with a frightening lack of awareness of what your real story is all about. No wonder you suffer from such crippling fears, childish dependencies, and a widespread lack of love for your own bodies.

If you want to set all that right, you must stop running away from the reality that you have been authentically human as embodied creatures of the earth for over six million years. Please try to grasp the big picture, and, having grasped it, please try to honor it. For my part, both I and my relational matrix have been unambiguously with you, on your evolving journey, throughout that entire time. We have affirmed and blessed every move you made with a total unmitigated "Yes." Assuredly, you are not perfect, and sometimes you did get it badly wrong, but I and my relational matrix can cope with that. For the greater part of the story you have done well; from our point of view there is much more on which we want to commend you rather than condemn you.

So back to incarnation—quite literally! Yes, incarnation! It did not begin with my earthly indwelling of two thousand years ago. It began six million years ago when you first began to evolve as a human species. Don't I remember it well! What a whale of time I and my relational matrix had, another erotic highlight—an incredible orgasm—in the birthing forth of unconditional love. Everything about it felt right, even the birth pangs! A wonderful, wonderful moment!

My coming in your flesh, blood, bone, and body was total and complete. And I have been in solidarity with you right through those six million years down to this very day. An incredibly moving story, and for me at least it is inconceivable that you seem to know so little about your very own story.

Now let me deviate for a few moments, just to remind you that the first five million years of your existence happened in what today you call *Africa*. As I reminded you at the beginning of the story, Africa is your primal and original home, the birthplace of the human species. Tell me, folks, why have you so outlandishly neglected your collective home? Why have you allowed it to be so battered and bruised by oppression and exploitation? If your home is in such a painful state, is it any wonder that there is so much alienation and meaningless suffering around the planet? Humans, wake up, your incarnational home needs your urgent and loving attention!

Now, if the relational matrix was fully with you in that original breakthrough into authentic humanity—six million years ago—why do you confine the notion of incarnation to my earthly indwelling of the past two thousand years? You seem to have problems with thinking big, and thinking deeply. You get stuck in the mire of imposed reductionism, with its insatiable desire for absolute control, not just over you but over me as well!

For some years now, wise people from your own ranks have been trying to tell you that your own species is engaged in a new evolutionary breakthrough, the likes of which happens only every few million years. Thus far, your unfolding has been largely of a biological nature. It has taken all this time to bring your biological growth to maturity. For me, and the relational matrix, we take our time with these substantial matters; it also means we savor the joy and mystery in a more real way!

So now your biological development as a species has reached a high point. From a purely biological viewpoint you can't really evolve much further. For the future, it will be psychic development rather than physical growth that will characterize your emergence.

That is what my earthly indwelling was all about. I was sent by the relational matrix to affirm and confirm all that had transpired in your great story for over six million years. That great story had to be celebrated, and the programme I developed to mark those wonderful achievements is what I called *the Kingdom of God!*

You mean to say . . .

JOACHIM: Teacher, you confuse me at times, and also make me downright angry. I'm an old man now, hoping for a home in heaven. I am hearing all this for the first time. Why weren't we told this years ago?

JOSHUA: Joachim, everything has its time and season. Maybe your people were not ready for it years ago.

JOACHIM: But why did your earthly indwelling happen two thousand years ago. Why didn't you wait until the people would be ready?

JOSHUA: Perhaps they needed the two thousand years to become ready. I guess we're dealing with one of the mysteries of evolution, in which things unfold often at a pace that does not make sense to us humans. And that's okay! The wise Spirit of my relational matrix knows what she's about!

JOACHIM: Well, I wish she would travel a bit more at our pace!

JOSHUA: If that were the case, Joachim, there would be no place for people like you. The young would have all the answers and all the robotic solutions, and there would be no place for the wisdom of the elders. It's the wisdom of the elderly that helps us to unravel the patterns that at times baffle and confuse us.

JOACHIM: There isn't much demand these days for the wisdom of the elders.

JOSHUA: I know—and civilization is all the poorer for that! But, Joachim, the current population is a rapidly aging one, and in a matter of a few decades, the elderly will come into their own—I am looking forward to that time.

JOACHIM: Well, I won't be around to see it!

JOSHUA: Would you like to put a bet on that? You have already made a big contribution to what is to come. Your living spirit will there. You wait and see!

The psychic energy of the future is very much a gift that the elderly will bring us! The day of the hard graft, with the focus on materiality, is undergoing a massive transformation. The future story is all about growth in mind and spirit (the psychic dimension). That is why I laid the foundations for you to engage in a new way with the wisdom of the creative Spirit of my relational matrix. From here on it is not the embodied presence of the matrix that is of primary significance but the psychic presence.

I thought I had made that abundantly clear when I told you that, in my embodied form, I had to depart, so that the Spirit could come afresh and lead you into the fullness of truth for this time of transition. And that is what the experience of resurrection also points toward, not something unique or different about me, but your humanity refashioned in the direction of psychic rather than physical potentiality.

Of course, this movement of my relational matrix is not confined to the Christian religion. This incarnational transformation happens globally. Each of the religions encapsulates the idea in a way that is congruent with their limited spiritual vision: the avatars of Hinduism, the bodhisattvas of Buddhism, the prophets of Islam. Because all the religions are so conditioned by the desire for control, all have adopted notions of incarnation that are disturbingly reductionistic, sexist, and exclusive.

Conscious Love

None of these expressions, the Christian one included, really honors the unconditional love of my relational matrix. It is in the power of that love that we forever birth forth reality. Humans are one among several unique expressions of our creativity but not the master species. There is no such thing as a master species. Each is unique in its capacity to contribute—in a mutually interdependent way—to the growth of all life, including that of the cosmos. Humanity has a distinctive responsibility for drawing forth the conscious dimensions of creation, particularly at this new evolutionary juncture when consciousness itself is so central to our understanding of universal life.

So the birthing forth of my relational matrix is the fruit of unconditional love. From the beginning of your evolution, some six million years ago, we have loved you unconditionally, inviting you into a cocreative relationship so that together we can promote the power of that unconditional love. For you humans, that has not been an easy challenge, but you have responded admirably and you got it basically right for much of the time.

Unfortunately, in the last eight thousand years you have been stuck in a kind of a black hole, preoccupied with your own unworthiness and, consequently, largely blind to the fundamental goodness of everything else in creation. You have set yourselves up as the imperialists who think they can set the whole thing right. Fortunately, you yourselves are beginning to see through the folly of this misguided manipulation. Slowly and painfully, you are coming to your senses, outgrowing the dominant ideologies in which you have been embroiled for the last eight thousand years.

For you, of course, eight thousand years seems like a massive time span, and some of your members despair of ever getting things right again. Have no worries! For my relational matrix, eight thousand years is just a flash in the pan, as the saying goes. The fact that you have messed things up for much of that time is not something we are going to hold against you. We'll forgive you for what you have done to yourselves. We just hope that someday you will also be able to forgive yourselves, because without that you won't be able to reclaim the power of unconditional love—and that's when you could find yourselves in very deep water, with species extinction staring you in the face!

Just as we love unconditionally everything in creation, from the beginning of your evolution, we have also loved you unconditionally. Through good times and bad, in your successes and failures—and you have succeeded more often than you have failed—we have loved and sustained you. Together we have birthed forth some marvelous possibilities, especially as creation at large matures into new levels of cosmic consciousness. It is in you humans, more than in any other creature, that this consciousness has become visible and transparent. You are creation becoming conscious of itself through the power of self-reflexive thought, which you manifest uniquely, but you have got to start manifesting it in a more *adult* way.

This gives you a capacity for wisdom unique among all creatures. You need to keep it closely aligned, however, to unconditional love. This is where things have gone badly wrong these last few thousand years. Your wisdom became very rational, mechanistic, imperialistic, and childishly immature. It was serving the love of power rather than the power of love. Now once more you need to call yourselves to conversion, individually and collectively. Forsake the hunger for power, and take the risk of learning to love once more!

Poetic Echoes . . .

The problem with the body is our problem with much else:
We regard it as an object to subdue.
But in essence, it's a process that begets an open space,
Inviting our engagement in the new.

The body takes its meaning from within and from without,
Belonging to a larger entity.
The cosmos is a body and planet earth as well.
On us humans, they confer identity.

The body of the human emerges from the flow
Of creation's pregnant yearning to become.
And the birthing of creation reveals the Deity,
In nature's great variety all abloom.

The channel through which Spirit inspires the cosmic soul
Is the form of the body so diverse.
Without embodied creatures, creation's elegance
Would fail the radiant beauty so intense.

It's the source of so much pleasure and the cause of so much pain.
It's perplexing and intriguing in design.
It's the icon of the breakthrough from beginning 'til the end.
The epitome of all that is divine.

Despise not then the body—of creatures or the earth.
Pervert not the justice to evoke.
The wholesome preconditions in which the body thrives.
For everything is destined for new growth.

Episode Fifteen

Birthing through Justice

L EARNING HOW TO LOVE RIGHTLY, that is, unconditionally, is an important prerequisite for a more meaningful future, not just for humanity but for the whole of creation. Now, one of the consequences of right loving is right relationships: with self, others, creation, and my relational matrix. And one of the core ingredients of relating rightly is the ability to work for justice.

All the religions tend to exalt love, but they don't include justice very often. Love without justice becomes a deceptive façade promising hope and meaning but rarely delivering. Justice is that strategy that translates the ideals into action, that grounds the hope by liberating new possibility.

Dignity and Value

Justice making is the invitation and challenge to treat each other and everything around you with dignity and value. In the cosmic scope of creation you see reflected the creative dynamics of my relational matrix. There are a number of obvious factors involved in this unceasing process:

1. Eros

This is the primal energy I spoke about earlier. The Spirit force of our relational matrix keeps a close eye on this creativity, ensuring that it always flows in a generative way, to the benefit of everything in creation. This is the force of passion, exuberance, and vitality. It is the dynamic energy that augments and sustains connectedness. It is the lure of every dream and visionary possibility. In your human lives you know this force primarily through your sexuality.

Oh dear, this is another gift you humans have not handled well.

You have invented so many phobias and hang-ups about sex! Why can't you simply enjoy it and stop making such a fuss about it.

2. Birthing

This is how the erotic moves forth by bringing into being embodied organisms ranging from stars to galaxies, landmasses, organic creatures, and the vast biodiversity that beautifies creation. My relational matrix gets such joy and fulfillment from this birthing-forth! This is the dimension where you humans need to refocus your energy right now. Much of what you birth forth, especially through technology and marketing forces is not justice producing. Many of you—particularly those among you who tend to hoard power and dominion for yourselves—inflict horrendous pain and suffering on so many impoverished people and on the embattled earth itself. This is not birth giving (natality); this is the diminution that leads to meaningless death (mortality).

3. Networking

Everything that is newly born, whether a star, planet, organic creature, or even a simple bacterium, needs a supportive environment, not just to survive but to realize the potential intended by my relational matrix. In other words, it needs a network of relations that supports the unfolding process of growth and possibility. This is the network of creative cooperation that scholars have noted in the bacterial world—going back some four billion years. Yes, this is a type of imprint beautifully reflecting the inner dynamics of my relational matrix.

4. Political Reform

I am quite overwhelmed by the array of political systems that you tolerate in today's world. Very few of them are democratic in any meaningful sense, and most of them are blatantly corrupt. Yet you go on voting them into power, colluding with their manipulation and at times reinforcing their addiction for domination and control. Your way of doing politics is totally unsustainable and causes tremendous pain to yourselves and to your earth. You can't have any meaningful sense of justice while you cling to the political regimes you currently support.

5. Ritual

As a species you seem to have lost the ability to mobilize people to liberating political engagement; correspondingly you have lost the capacity to mobilize the creativity for political praxis. Ritual making arises from the need and desire to celebrate significant experiences in life. The rational mind cannot apprehend reality in its fullness; indeed, it can only access reality in a very limited way. The governing principle of relationality, which is the primal energy of every experience, requires interactive processes that draw on imagination and creativity. Without this ritual outlet, life shrivels up and can easily become absorbed in nihilism.

Revamping the Vision

You have really lost your bearings on this issue which is so central to the New Reign of God. You associate justice with just wages, just rights (and rarely speak of *duties*), just war (in my opinion, there is no such thing), just working practices, justice for the poor and marginalized by giving generously in time of need. In recent years you talk about justice for the earth and for creation, what you call eco-justice or geo-justice.

In its basic meaning, justice-making is about all those practices that give priority to right relationships in every sphere of life. And right relationship means a way of relating that is empowering and liberating for the earth and for every creature inhabiting it. Consequently, you can't have right relationships in an earth fragmented into nation-states, rival ethnic groups, and competing religions. Neither can you have right relationships when you adopt imperial-style governments, economies based on exploitation of the earth's resources, educational systems based on fierce competition, and a philosophy of life rending things asunder around the dualistic divisions of sacred versus secular, body versus spirit, mind versus matter, God versus humankind.

To begin with, you need to take justice completely out of the religious systems. The religions are too immersed in oppressive regimes to be able to deliver justice. Justice needs to become the primary concern of those who seek to govern humanity and its relation to the earth. That suggests that it is the primary responsibility of politicians and economists. I see no possibility of their taking on this challenge. Therefore, it falls to you, the people. You need to become subversive and prophetic, as I was in my earthly indwelling, particularly in my commitment to the New Reign of God. You have the blueprint there—the rest is up to you.

I see two crucial strategies, one related to thinking and the other to organizing. You need to learn to think differently, so that you can see in greater depth. You need that big vision I have alerted you to so often in this story. You need to think inclusively, and above all be sure to include the cosmos and the home planet. You need to think relationally and forsake all this crazy adversarial conditioning in which you are so indoctrinated. And you need a lot of silence, just to be and connect with the heart; otherwise you will waste a lot of creative energy.

In terms of organization, you need to set in motion a whole series of networks—small, reflective, creative groups where people will gather around critical issues, where every voice can be heard, and where proactive engagement can be activated. Don't be waiting for politicians and those who govern you; they can't deliver on what is of central importance either for people or for the earth. We need on a global scale a politics of people-power, but please, please, please, remember it has to be a power of service not of domination.

And keep before your minds that everything you encounter is *gift*. Therefore treat everything with care and gentleness. And don't be greedy and hoarding. There is plenty for everybody—my relational matrix has made sure of that. And call forth in each other the *adult*, so that we move with creation into a new phase where true growth can happen and people can learn once more what it really means to live.

You mean to say . . .

NELSON: But, Sir, that is so far-fetched, we'd be wasting our time even thinking about it.

JOSHUA: Well, you come up with a better proposition.

NELSON: We need to try to reform the existing systems.

JOSHUA: A lot of sweat and blood have already been spilled try-

ing to reform something that is effectively beyond reform.
All the major institutions you humans have invented are in
decline. They are passing away, let them die!

POLICEMAN: Sounds like you are advocating anarchy. Law and
order are already enough of a headache for us, with prisons
so overcrowded we have no place to put criminals anymore.

JOSHUA: Precisely the point I was making. The system is breaking
down and the breakdown cannot be contained by the conventional methods.

POLICEMAN: But we'll have worse problems if we go along with
your ideas.

JOSHUA: No you won't! People are deeply frustrated because the
prevailing world order is not liberating life for people or
indeed for any other creature that inhabits universal life. The
prevailing system is fundamentally flawed.

NELSON: We call it original sin.

JOSHUA: Forget about original sin. That explanation has been
tested and has proved a dismal failure. It disempowers people instead of empowering people to engage more coherently
and creatively.

NELSON: But, Sir, if I do the things you advocate I could end up
being arrested and even put in prison.

POLICEMAN: Have no fear, mate; all the goddamned prisons are
full to capacity!

JOSHUA: Nelson, be not afraid. They will revile you and persecute
you and utter all sorts of false words against you. They will
drag you before governors and judges and tribunals. But
hold your head high, because the work you're about is the
task of liberation.

Networking for Justice

I want to say a few more things bout *networking*, because, I guess,
this is quite a new idea to many of you. Networking thrives on a
kind of free-for-all where creativity, trust, and mutual collaboration
are the key ingredients whereby people can draw forth each other's
gifts and resources and empower one another for the mutual benefit of all. But that is impossible in many of the governing institutions

you have evolved in recent millennia, institutions where the resourcefulness is invested and hoarded by the ruling few to the detriment of the many who feel disempowered and impoverished. This is also the realm where convoluted arguments unfold, claiming to be rendering service to others when in fact the real goal is the accumulation of wealth and power for the ruling few.

In fact, in all sorts of quiet and unassuming ways, millions of people, especially among the poor, beaver away at it, often against the heavy odds of manipulation and domination. It is difficult to have real networking on an earth that has been fragmented into tribal rivalries, ethnic divisions, and especially into nation-states. It is so alien to everything my relational matrix symbolizes. Planet Earth is a unified organism that thrives on creativity and diversity. The problem with the nation-state is that it militates against both the unity and the diversity. It fragments the inherent unity and undermines the rich diversity in order to enforce its own hegemony.

You mean to say . . .

RULER: But, Sir, our nation was given to us by God. It is our chosen land. And we rule over it as God commanded, just as other peoples rule over their nations.

JOSHUA: Nation-states are a human invention and are of very recent origin. For well over 90 percent of your time on the earth you knew nothing of such distinctions.

RULER: But people were primitive then, living in the darkness of sin and ignorance.

JOSHUA: Who said so?

RULER: Our faith tells us so, and so do all our great scholars.

JOSHUA: Yes, because it suits them to believe it; it validates their hunger for power.

RULER: But Adonai gave us that power, to rule and master the world on his behalf.

JOSHUA: The divine power you refer to is a projection of your own fascination with power. My relational matrix, from which all creation emanates, never knew such power. What we are concerned about is the power of empowering. That's what I mean when I talk about justice-making.

RULER: But Adonai is the source of all justice.

JOSHUA: Not quite! My relational matrix is the source of all justice, and therefore you can't have justice until you learn to relate in a way that is about building things up rather than fragmenting life into entities like nation-states.

RULER: But then, who is going to be in charge?

JOSHUA: Creation will be in charge, and there is a great urgency for us humans to learn how to be at the service of creation and at the service of each other.

RULER: I don't like it; I like to know where I stand with things!

Why can't you humans live with this one undivided earth that you have known for over 90 percent of your time here? Why this compulsion of breaking everything down in this violent process of divide and conquer? If you want to create planetary subsections to augment the networking why not develop *bio-regions* that respect the earth's own natural constellations of energy and resources rather than those superficial anthropocentric divisions you call nation-states?

Ritualizing for Justice

The commitment to justice making needs to be sustained by rituals that inspire, on the one hand, and call people to accountability, on the other. As a species, you have known the skills and wisdom of good ritual for several thousands of years. You illustrated this graphically in the way you buried the dead about one hundred thousand years ago. Meanwhile, churches and religions have largely robbed you of this capacity, but deep in your hearts you know how to do it. And look to your indigenous peoples all over the world, especially in Africa, who still facilitate some wonderfully inspiring rituals.

In your ritual celebrations, honor once more the earth, its cycles, seasons, and gifts to humanity. Cultivate wisdom and respect for how we treat the earth, the other creatures, and one another. Celebrate all that comes to birth and all that evolves through the cycle of death and rebirth. Heal the sick, look after the poor, care for the refugees, and make sure that nobody is ever isolated or alienated because of need.

And never let the sun go down on your anger. So much damage has been done and so much hurt caused in these competitive "battles" that you are forever waging. You even wage war with your own inner selves, pushing your bodies and spirits in the battle to be better than everyone else. Ironically, you then end up battling with all the chronic illnesses you bring upon yourselves. You certainly got yourselves into a senseless mess. Yet it can be rectified and healed, if people would only learn how to be vulnerable and humble. The major challenges—indeed the one that is foundational to many others—is that you humans wake up to who you really are and reclaim your rightful place within the living web of creation.

Much needs to be done at the human level to promote reconciliation between rich and poor, black and white, friend and enemy. However, these issues will remain largely unresolved until we all become reconciled with the cosmos and with our primordial home on planet earth. That is where all justice making begins, and that too is its culmination, namely, to come back home to where we truly and primarily belong and reclaim our legitimate place with integrity, love, and truth. You can't hope to heal the wounds of poverty, racism, oppression, and violence until a new reconciliation begins to happen with the earth and cosmic bodies. With that basic aspect in place, then, there are enduring foundations on which a more creative future can be constructed.

I appreciate your patience while I spoke about this subject, so close to my heart and to that of my relational matrix. All the talk about love gets us nowhere until we get involved in changing our world in the direction of justice. Formidable though the task may be, it is one of the non-negotiables! The other major one is contemplation. They are two sides of the same coin. In a word, you see my face most clearly as you gaze into the eyes of the African person dying of AIDS and every fiber of your being cries out in anguish and in passion because you know that this is a reflection of a world tortured by injustice. The very experience drives you into action, and it is precisely in that action that I am with you now, and will be until the end of time. Amen.

Poetic Echoes . . .

(L= Lionel; J=Joshua)

L. *I reckon 'twould take me a number of months*
    To build all the sheds that I need.
    And then, I could store all the goods I possess
    My cattle, my trucks and my seed.

J. *Now listen, young man, just give it a thought.*
    What gain from all this you expect?
    You can't take it with you and apart from all that
    You're fleecing the poor of their rent.

L. *I worked hard in life and kept all the rules,*
    "Compete and win where you can."
    If they all worked like me—and all of them can
    Then, we'd all have a place on the land.

J. *Young man, you don't see the deeper design,*
    The gift that we all share is one.
    It's not yours or mine to portion at will
    Nor hoard to your satisfaction.

L. *To master the land is man's unique task,*
    To conquer and subdue creation.
    It's there for our use, so for God's sake wake up
    And honor the faith of your nation.

J. *Young man, I'm beyond the nation-estate*
    My home is creation's dominion.
    Where justice can thrive in fairness to all
    And no one's deprived of an earning.

L. *Well, sadly, Good Sir, I cannot espouse,*
    You're sounding a bit communistic.
    We live at a time when life's insecure.
    I'm sorry if I sound pessimistic.

J. *At times, it's not easy to make the right choice,*
    When justice requires our attention.
    Together we hold a gift to be shared.
    It needs our discerning protection.

Episode Sixteen

Birthing a New Reign of Radical Inclusiveness

O F ALL THE NOTIONS I came up with during my earthly indwelling, probably the idea of the Kingdom of God was the most innovative. I have already talked to you about it and explained why I chose the kingly kind of language, which I know feels out of place for many of you today. Let me just mention again what the key bit is for me, then and now: *radical inclusiveness.*

Whereas human-designed kingships tend to be structured on elitist principles of who is in and who is not allowed in, who ranks above or below, who can access the privileges of office and who can't, in my kingly vision all that is toppled on its head. While earthly kingships condone, and at times promote, a reign of power and glory, a reign of wealth, a reign of terror, a reign of prosperity, my "upside-down kingdom" is about a reign of radical inclusiveness, where power becomes the prerogative of the powerless, where the marginalized know they belong, and where true liberation is offered to everybody.

Here you can see as clearly as I can make it what my relational matrix is all about. This is the secret to living rightly; this is the prescription for true holiness. This is the vision of the divine, not ensconced in some faraway heaven, to which the good ones will escape someday, but immersed in the heart of living reality, calling forth a new order of egalitarian participation in the task of making all things new. My sense of how that might happen in your time is what I want to explore with you today.

No Outcasts Anymore

Let me begin with the *inclusiveness.* To put it most simply and directly, it means that everything and everybody is included; therefore, nothing is excluded anymore. Could it be simpler? But, yes, there are obstacles, and many of you know what they are. We who have been so well brainwashed about who to like and not to like, who to rub shoulders with and who to avoid, who to love and who to hate, my friends, all that we must leave behind us now. We're in a new time, with new challenges awaiting our commitment and devotion.

You mean to say . . .

ANGOLAN WOMAN: In my culture, this is not going to work. The men are in charge and we are all expected to respect them. They say where women can go and can't go. And if you break the rules you become a complete outcast.

JOSHUA: You can't be a complete outcast, because you won't be excluded from my relational matrix, nor from the earth nor the cosmos.

WOMAN: But I have to live with my people. There is no point talking to them about planets and cosmos and new ways of relating.

JOSHUA: I am sure you are not the only person in your culture feeling as you do. Even if there are only a few others, you can begin conversations among yourselves and explore the possibility of setting up small support groups of those who think differently.

WOMAN: But that won't do anything to change the men who rule the villages or the missionaries who support them.

JOSHUA: Okay, initially it won't change them, but it will change you. And transformative change tends to come from the ground up as *adult* people like you take responsibility for self-empowerment and the mutual empowerment of those ready to come on board.

WOMAN: That could be a long, slow process.

JOSHUA: I agree, a bit like the mustard seed I talked about during my earthly indwelling, but in the rapidly changing world of this time, transformation can happen in leaps and bounds. Sometimes a small seed can produce an amazing shrub. And better begin small rather than not begin at all.

WOMAN: Thanks for your encouragement; I hope it will work.

JOSHUA: Hold firmly to your hope and the chances are that it will work!

The other aspect that you must not neglect is that the Kingdom is not just about people. It is very much—perhaps primarily—about systems and structures, beginning with nothing less than the cosmos itself. How do we embrace what our cosmos is about, in all its elegance and grandeur? This is the primordial womb of belonging, which also must be included. Either things belong here or they have no existence. This is the primary abode of my relational matrix. This is the nourishing womb of all possibility, through which my relational matrix has been birthing forth for aeons long past and for aeons yet to come.

The Realm of Belonging

In a sense you can't relate rightly with my New Reign until you first relate to the whole of creation. This is the organism that begets every atom and molecule, every star and planet, every bacterium and termite, every plant, fish, animal, and human. This is the biggest embrace we have ever known, beautifully depicted in the curved nature of space-time. In this sacred space, everybody and everything has its place, a place of welcome, warmth, and hospitality—and, yes, a place where possibilities unfold according to the paradoxical mixture of creation and destruction.

It is not perfect, and it never has been. But that's not a problem, at least not for me and the relational matrix. I know humans get very screwed up over the misadventures of nature and the imponderables that will not submit to the rationality of the human mind. What you humans need to change is yourselves and your distorted minds, not the landscape of creation. Reclaim your indigenous wisdom whereby, for several thousand years, you befriended and ritualized the creation in its birthing forth of life through birth and death, through growth and decay. You did this so coherently and spiritually until zealously confused missionaries desecrated so much that was sacred to you. Creation is fine if people would only honor its inherent wisdom. In your native rituals you have much of the wisdom to treat creation in a sacred way and thus enhance the work of my relational matrix.

So that is the first challenge for the inclusiveness of the Kingdom. People need to wake up to realize the enormity, complexity, and beauty of the universe to which we all belong. That is the primary revelation upon which every disclosure, divine and human, can be postulated. Only when we come home to our cosmic belonging, cherishing it in its prodigious endowment and embracing it in all the diversity of its light and shadow, do we stand any realistic hope of advancing to the new evolutionary moment now impending upon our world.

Pure Gift

I had a terrible time during my earthly indwelling explaining to my disciples, especially the men, that the New Reign I was inaugurating was offered as pure gift to everybody. I laid down no conditions. It was there for the taking, and they just could not get their heads around that notion. They were so conditioned by the culture of brokering, whereby everything had to be earned and obtained at a price. It blew their minds completely.

You mean to say . . .

INDIAN DALIT: But, Teacher, it totally baffles me also. Most times I have to go down on my two knees like a beggar. Had I not done that many times, my children would have starved to death.

JOSHUA: I understand what you are saying, and I know something of your pain and anguish. You see, that is why I emphasize the bigger picture of creation so much. Creation bestows abundantly, but humans have taken on this strange habit of hoarding. If they would only honor what creation is about, then your integrity and dignity would also be honored.

INDIAN: No, Sir, it wouldn't make a difference because I belong to the lowest caste.

JOSHUA: But there is no such thing as caste in creation; it is
humans who invented that disgusting notion.

DALIT: But the leaders of my people say that this is God's will
and that we should accept it.

JOSHUA: Now that is what I call *blasphemy*. You do NOT accept
it. In fact, you denounce it every opportunity you get, and
you need to mobilize your people into small subversive
groups to begin changing the consciousness that validates
such disgusting oppression.

DALIT: Easy for you to say; you are a man and you won't have to
deal with the wrath of their disapproval.

JOSHUA: In my earthly indwelling, I did become the victim of
what you rightly call the "wrath of their disapproval."
Unfortunately that is the price we sometimes have to pay to
bring about the New Reign. I will be with you in the Spirit
of solidarity; do not be afraid!

Yes, it is a gift given in radical freedom, and therefore offered to
everybody without conditions. And this then becomes the paradox,
indeed a cruel paradox for so many oppressed peoples in our world,
and for the oppressed Earth itself: if this is a free gift why do we
deprive each other of it. Who gave any of us that right? Who even
gave us the right to lay down conditions?

This is where I really want to reassure you and ask you not to
submit to despair. When you realize that the message of my earthly
indwelling has made so little difference over two thousand years,
then it is all too easy to throw in the towel. First, as I have said so
many times, the message is bigger than me; it belongs essentially to
my relational matrix, and nothing can stop the power of my relational matrix. Second, on the grand scale of things, two thousand
years is a very short time, although I know it feels massive when you
are down in the dumps. Let me assure you there is still hope. Liberation is close at hand.

Engaging the Powers

That brings me to the crux of my message on the Kingdom. I am
horrified at how some of the churches have spiritualized this idea,

and instead of keeping the main focus on my New Reign, many of the churches themselves have assumed center stage. As long as the church is successful as they understand it, then they assume the Kingdom is flourishing. Sadly, that is far from being the case, and here I need to make a few things clear.

I never equated church with Kingdom of God. In fact in my earthly indwelling I was not that interested in, nor worried about, what you people call *church*. That is why I keep bringing you back to the context of my relational matrix, for which the whole of creation is the primary consideration. All the religions fail to honor that big vision. In one way or another they all subvert the breadth and depth of our vision of birthing forth new life.

When it comes to church, you got sucked into this same reductionistic strategy. My friend Paul set you a wonderful example, but that, too, you have not honored. He traveled around to the infant Christian communities, helping them to form faith communities around my vision: small, creative, flexible groups, focused on worship and service, and not overly concerned about structure or procedure. That's exactly what the vision of the New Reign is about; that's precisely how my relational matrix promotes growth and liberation.

Friends, you will eventually have to get rid of these big imperial-like institutions, with all the regalia, pomposity, and legalism that goes with them. They have nothing to do with me, nor my vision.

You mean to say . . .

BISHOP: Come on now, Teacher, don't be jumping on the band-wagon of all this postmodernist, laissez-faire propaganda. The church has not been perfect, but look at all it has achieved. The good far exceeds the limitations.

JOSHUA: My good friend, the good happened in spite of, rather than because of, the church. Creation itself is destined for goodness, and the good will win out in the end, church or no church.

BISHOP: You really do exaggerate!

JOSHUA: Not really. What I am saying is that the good the church achieved was brought about because creation itself—mysteriously—draws forth good, even when the dominant structures are patently evil.

BISHOP: Now please, Sir, you are not going to compare the church to an evil structure are you?

JOSHUA: Not only the church, but all the religions have left the world with a lot of meaningless pain and suffering, with bloodshed in the name of truth and inquisitions in the name of control.

BISHOP: But you are forgetting what the church has done for the poor and marginalized around the world.

JOSHUA: The church has helped the poor and marginalized to survive, but not exactly to thrive, which is what my New Reign is about. And I find the church (and indeed, all the religions) very weak at challenging the systemic structures that cause the poor to be poor in the first place and that also prevent true liberation from taking place.

BISHOP: But that's the task of governments and politicians, not the function or purpose of the church.

JOSHUA: In my New Reign, there is no place for dualisms. For my relational matrix, creation is one—religionists and politicians must learn to work together if true liberation is to be brought about.

BISHOP: So, in a word, do you see a future for the church?

JOSHUA: Yes, I do, vibrant communities of faith that call forth the adult in people; networks that generate hope and fresh possibility—not insipid institutions where the living Spirit is often smothered and crushed.

The vision of my New Reign focuses on right relationships, not just in a religious or church context but in fidelity to the creative energy of my relational matrix. This is not a matter of getting it right with God, nor just among people. To get relationships right requires engagement with ecology, politics, economics, social policy. Every human-designed structure and system has to be called to accountability. All contribute to make the relationships right, and if they are not contributing, then they are hindering the process.

I have already spoken of the need for a new way of doing politics beyond the dualisms of church versus state, religious versus secular, spiritual versus political. I abhor these binary distinctions. They have caused so much division, disempowerment, and meaningless suffering. They bolster up the disintegrating cultural edifice, desperately clinging to its past power and glory. This is not the way forward. This is not the vision of my New Reign. This is not the basis on which you can build adult faith communities for the future.

I am now doing a new thing, like water oozing into desert places. I need you there with me and with the relational matrix, awakening once more a yearning for that love and justice which embrace everything in the unfolding plan of creation.

Assuredly, we'll meet opposition and misunderstanding, slander and blackmailing. But we need to hold our heads high, because we are about the task of liberation—and this time around, it must not be compromised!

Poetic Echoes . . .

    D. *I never felt so much out of place.*
        Sturdy pillars of ancient granite.
        Stained-glass windows of holy heroic people.
        Pinewood benches oozing the odor of sanctity.
        Creaking floorboards echoing the divine ache.
        O God, be merciful to me, a sinner!

        And look at him, with his hands aloft,
        Praising Adonai for the gift of grace.
        He glances at the checklist;
        This time the reckoning looks good.
        And yes, I agree, he has a right to be chuffed.
        But—O God, be merciful to me, a sinner!

        Hey! Hold on a moment, why am I here?
        I have not been in this place for years.
        Tax collectors are barred from here.
        The boundaries are clear and so are the rules.
        I have intruded upon sacred space.
        O God, be merciful to me, a sinner!

Hey, you, Joshua, what's going on?
You took me by the hand and brought me here.
You, a Jew, breaking your own sacred laws!
Do you realize the risk you're taking?
And what's the purpose of all this anyhow?
O God, be merciful to both of us—sinners!

J. *Brother Damien, welcome to the new dispensation.*
The barriers have all been removed.
The rules have all been broken.
Unconditional love has overtaken us all,
And there is room for you, for me, and even for him,
Yes, God is merciful to us sinners!

And Damien, the sinner now becomes the catalyst.
Let all enjoy true freedom!
There's a New Reign, a new dispensation.
Unconditional love is the law of the land.
No outsiders anymore; all are in now.
O God, be merciful to those who keep people outside!

EPISODE SEVENTEEN

'Til We Meet Again!

SO, THERE YOU ARE, my friends, we are on our way and what a wonderful way it is! Not easy—but deep in our hearts, we know it is right. And don't get distracted by all this shortsighted preoccupation about the end! Because, friends, there is no end! Your earthly existence will come and go, just as mine did. I live on, and so do you! Everything lives on in a creative universe like ours. Subatomic particles cannot be destroyed; they are always transformed into another form of energy. And energy carries information, the cumulative wisdom of the ages.

Living with Infinity

You mean to say . . .

EMMA: But, Teacher, in the Gospels there are several references to the end of the world. In fact, all the religions seem to consider it very important.

JOSHUA: Emma, religion really never came to terms with the meaning of creation. None of the religions, including the fourteen hundred that have been perpetuated in my name take creation seriously, as my relational matrix wishes. Religion is forever trying to escape into this mythic beyond, which simply does not exist.

TIMOTHY: And, Sir, what about all the references to the second coming? Will you not come back again?

JOSHUA: Timothy, I never left, so how could I come back? And what would I come back for?

TIMOTHY: To be more truly present among us.

JOSHUA: But I cannot be more radically present than I already am in the power of the living Spirit of my relational matrix.

EMMA: So what should we tell people about the end of the world, and judgment, and reward hereafter? You know for many people these are the really important issues.

JOSHUA: Yes, I know, people live with such fear. You see, religion has prevented people from really being at home in creation in a way that would make my relational matrix so much more real and transparent. Then the focus would not be on afterlife, judgment, and all those other morbid issues. The focus would be on the unfolding of creation itself, and the call to each and every one of us to be fully involved. Basically, we judge ourselves to the degree to which we do or do not participate in that process.

EMMA: And the end of the world?

JOSHUA: It's of no interest to me, and neither is all that speculation about the beginning. You see, Emma, the idea of something having a beginning and ending is a human preoccupation. It is humans who need those categories, and

they need them in order to feel in control of reality. But creation is in control of itself, and does not need those anthropocentric boundaries. My relational matrix works with
horizons that forever grow and expand, not with boundaries
that keep things closed and static.

TIMOTHY: So, how do we make sense of the future, or do we
have a future at all?

JOSHUA: Of course, you have a future, one that is full of hope
and promise, provided you trust what is unfolding all
around you and stop playing this meaningless game of dominance and control.

My friends, as you emerge from the oppressive power that has
entrapped you, you will discover once more what intuitively you
knew so well for thousands of years. This is a wise universe; ours is
a wise earth. Both have been receptive to the power of Wisdom for
aeons past, and indeed will be for aeons yet to come. Strange isn't it
that the wise and holy Spirit of my relational matrix had no great
problem with the stars and galaxies, with the bacteria and the animals!

So, why are you humans behaving in this strangely stubborn and
unenlightened way!

Look around you and contemplate the wonder of all that exists in
creation. Everything works in cooperative fashion as it is designed
to do; and I say cooperative, and within that cooperative endeavor
is a great deal of freedom and choice. You do have the capacity for
greater choice, what your scholars call free will, but, unfortunately,
in recent millennia you have not used it very freely, and certainly not
creatively. Part of the problem is that you got locked into this notion
that you are the end of the evolutionary line, that the whole thing
stops with you, and that therefore you are masters of the whole she-
bang! Well, I'm sorry to disappoint you, but that on that score, you
have got it about as wrong you could possibly have got it!

The whole point of relationality is that it has no end. It is not a
linear stretch with a beginning and end. It is much more ethereal and
magical. Fortunately, some of your scientists, exploring string theory, are beginning to get it these days. Yes, this creation closely
resembles a musical instrument being tuned into higher vibrations,

and when those vibrations begin to weave together we have the orchestra of creation, elegantly reflecting the power of my relational matrix. Strings and loops and membranes—that's the stuff it is all made of; don't worry too much about the fine details, especially all the speculation about the eleven dimensions of the space-time continuum; some evening as I watch a beautiful sunset, I might try and work that one out for myself!

Vision for the Future

For the way ahead, I suggest you keep a close eye on three things: contemplation, right relations, and justice-making. Look at the birds of the air, they labor not and do not spin, yet they know they are loved and cherished. Stretch your narrow little minds and think big. You weren't given brains just to cram for exams, to build nuclear weapons, or accumulate money and power. Your brain is a dimension of your body that itself belongs to the earth body, in turn to the cosmic body, and ultimately to my relational matrix.

You need to marvel at and contemplate the mystery and simply gaze at the wonder of it all. And you need to wonder too at the paradox through which it all hangs together. I know, at times, it looks weird to you humans. You don't like watching a lion tear a little zebra to pieces and neither do I. To be perfectly honest with you, I can't explain the rationale behind that. At a later stage in your evolution you'll be able to grasp its paradoxical meaning. For now, just learn to befriend the paradox!

Meanwhile, instead of worrying about the cruelty in nature, give your attention to all the cruelty you yourselves create. This is the meaningless suffering that petrifies you today, and there is no point in praying to me to resolve it for you. You are ADULTS; you created the mess, you go and sort it out! And I suggest you be particularly vigilant around the violence you have created. Much of it is subtle; all of it is systemic; and it is all wrapped up in the addiction to dominance and control.

We hope that a day will come when you can withdraw the destructive projections and withhold all the meaningless suffering you impose upon creation! You won't achieve this by invoking a theory of redemptive violence either in the name of the Christian cross or the Islamic *jihad*. I am not interested in either and I never was. You need to face the meaningless suffering that is largely a human-imposed phenomenon, and it is entirely up to you humans to resolve it. If you choose not to resolve it, then you have been told time and again how dire the consequences will be.

There is no point in waiting for me or some other heavenly figure to intervene. My relational matrix set everything in motion and endowed the whole thing with creative freedom. Everything in creation, including your own species, is more than adequately endowed for the task of living creatively and responsively—and for living meaningfully with the paradox of creation and destruction that characterizes the evolving process. The whole thing is so much bigger and more complex than you, humans.

Trying to control it is what has got you into such a mess, ironically a mess that could reap your own perdition. If you choose to destroy yourselves, I am not going to play the rescuing parent. You have got to grow up and become adults. There is no space for childish power games in my relational matrix.

It is not a case of trying to work it out in your heads. You humans spend far too much time in your heads, driving yourselves crazy with man-made reason and rationality. Get into your hearts and see with the eyes of deeper vision. That is what will give you hope and meaning. And thereby you'll access the wisdom that will enable you to live differently, with more love and compassion for all sentient beings.

So contemplation is the first move; easy to learn and to do for those who don't cling to everything! As you dwell deeply with reality, you'll get the message fairly quickly, the one I have stated over and over again during the narration of this story, namely, that relationality and right relationships are the clue to the whole meaning of life at every level. Keep your attention on learning to relate rightly: with the cosmos, with the earth, with all creatures inhabiting creation, and all will be well.

The fact that relationships are far from right in so many spheres is not creation's fault, nor that of my relational matrix. It is your fault, arising from the belligerent adolescent stage of your evolutionary growth. This is something you can change and modify, and you don't need to pray for the grace for that undertaking, because you have already been graced abundantly. There has never been a time in which my grace was not fully available to you.

As my friend Paul reminded you almost two thousand years ago, my grace is sufficient for you; in fact, for billions of years, it has been more than sufficient!

And as I said previously, you don't have to flagellate yourselves over the fact that you have made such a mess of things. In the big scale of creation, over several "billennia," your stupid behavior feels to me more of a nuisance than a hindrance. It just annoys me that it is taking you so long to grow up and become cosmic, planetary adults. Meanwhile, I and my relational matrix will forgive you for being such pests—not to me, but to the earth and to your own kind!

So, come on, folks, time is running short and Mother Earth is getting weary of all this adolescent belligerence. The hour is fast approaching when you will have to choose between life and extinction. The choice is yours. If you want to remain part of the creative evolving process, that will be great. If you choose not to, my relational matrix is not short of creative options—for the earth and the cosmos. If you choose to be within those options, that will be fantastic. If you choose to remain outside them, you will have doomed yourselves to extinction.

Frankly, I don't understand why you would want to do that. It saddens me to think that you might do it, and I would be treating you as robots if I intervened to rescue you from yourselves. So please wake up, and let's face a new dawn together. Let's wrap ourselves in the light of the rising sun, so that we can penetrate the anthropocentric darkness that is engulfing the earth at this time. Amen!

Poetic Echoes . . .

Death's a horizon we passed long ago
On the journey from here to the Cosmos.
We die to be born anew to the Source
Of creation's perpetual engagement.
I've been down that road—I know it too well
With its fears and foreboding concern.
The veil is so thin, between now and then,
One wonders why fear is so rampant.

The Spirit of life and the Spirit of death
Is one and the same intuition.
Our friendships endure and love is secure
In creation's embrace of the infinite.
Yes, I'm always so near, you never need care
Do not be afraid, I've oft spoken.
Relate in deep love and be well assured
The fullness of life's your endowment.

Beware of your stance in creation's great dance,
Remember its basic aliveness.
Do not dominate, control, nor inflate.
Instead, cocreate with endeavor.
And build up my Reign of justice and love.
Set free all who're trapped in illusion.
And greet each new day with a smile to convey
That you're loved without reserve forever.

Aftermath

December 26, 2004, has become one of those dates some of you will never forget. It was the day the tsunami devastated the coastlands of Southeast Asia, killing almost 250,000 people, ravaging hamlet, city, and natural habitat, and leaving millions forlorn and bewildered, angry and racked in pain.

Devotees of all the great religions, and even those who never took religion seriously, were united around one heart-rending question: What was the divine up to? Was this a punishment for sin and human waywardness? Why did God not intervene? And if God chose not to intervene what is this cruel and capricious game God is trying to play? Understandably some began to ask: Does the divine life-force exist at all?

The questions sound familiar, and yes, there are answers, but they belong to another way of seeing and understanding reality. Can you recall the disciples in my earthly indwelling asking about the Kingdom of God? They, too, expected rational answers! And I wish at times I could have offered them, but that would be a betrayal of my mission—and theirs as well. So, I opted for the parable—the great liberating story that turns the world upside down and liberates a truth the rational mind can never really comprehend.

A Parable for Our Time!

December 26, 2004, was like any other morning in Southeast Asia. For many people it was holiday time, and the bright warm sunshine invited them to paddle in the sea waters. And some people did observe that the waters had receded far from the shoreline, but few were able to interpret the hidden and alarming message.

One group of people did, the Morgan tribe of western Thailand. These gypsy fisher-folk were intrigued by the ebbing waters of their beloved shoreland. For centuries these living waters had nourished and sustained them. The aggravated activity of the fish suggested that the spirit of the waters was not at peace on this otherwise beautiful morning. In the power of their collective lore and intuitive wisdom they invoked the living Spirit of my relational matrix. They discerned that within a matter of hours the receding waters would return with a vengeance and crash mightily upon their shores. Having gathered their meager belongings, they retired to the mountains. None of their number was hurt or harmed.

And let me tell you another parable: About five hundred miles away, an island tribe was invoking the living Spirit to discern the erratic behavior of the local bird life. They, too, decided to shelter on higher ground. And they, too, were unharmed!

The gypsy fisher-folk did not try to play a control game. They surrendered to deeper wisdom. They listened; in fact, they listened very deeply. The might and wrath of nature could not, and did not, harm them. I tell you, there are many lessons to be learned from this story. Or, perhaps, you need to learn from the animal kingdom, most of whom were neither harmed nor killed by the tsunami. They, too, listened, and nature did not harm them. And you have the arrogance to think that you are higher than the animals! And some of you torture your inner souls trying to subdue and punish the animal within you. I suggest it is about time you learned to befriend it.

The Baffling Paradox

Okay, let me tell you a few things about earthquakes. Sure, even for me and the relational matrix they are baffling at times, but every time we witness one, we know that this is the Earth Mother in the birthpangs of new possibilities. Without earthquakes there would be no life on this beautiful planet earth: no fireflies, daffodils, rolling sea waters, art, music, or human beings. All would be arid and lifeless. It takes a destructive outburst to release pregnant energy! This is the great paradox I have alluded to so many times in my story. Without this paradox—of creation and destruction—there is no freedom, creativity, wonder, or mystery.

Many of the earthquakes are highly destructive of human life, but that is not of our making; it is the result of your ignorance and injustice. It is a human problem, not a divine one. Some of you have enough wealth and resources to build earthquake-resistant cities, and the loss of life tends to be minimal. Why don't you share those resources equally and justly? Then the poor need not be so scared of earthquakes, because they are the ones who usually suffer most. And if you refrain from pumping all sorts of pollutants into the upper atmosphere, hurricanes and tsunamis might not be so ferocious.

But, folks, there is nothing to be gained by blaming me or the relational matrix. We have empowered you with resources far beyond your current state of ignorance. And we have richly endowed you in freedom and creativity. Moreover, we have noticed how brilliant you are at charity in the face of massive disasters. But charity is only a small part of an authentic response. Charity in itself will not see you through. So, wake up and be alert! Creation is at a new critical evolutionary threshold and you'll need all the resilience you can muster to see yourselves through in a meaningful and liberating way!

Hope Survives!

And don't forget the fisher-folk! Rightly we remember the grief-stricken and broken-hearted, those who have lost everything, and those whose lives will never be the same again. And if they need anything to face the daunting future it is HOPE! Perhaps, it is they, more than anybody else, that need to look to the fisher-folk for the wisdom and courage to make a fresh start!

THE FIRST LETTER OF JOSHUA

To the Morgan Fisher-folk of Thailand!

Dear Friends,

On behalf of my relational matrix, I want to thank and complement you for your astuteness and depth of wisdom. When I see what you did on December 26, 2004, I know that Incarna-

tion has not been in vain! I know there is still hope for the human race, because dotted around the world are a few million people like you, enough to create the critical mass to see humanity through the evolutionary transition of this complex and bewildering time.

You are the midwives of this pregnant moment, an awesome responsibility indeed, but one you can shoulder with dignity and grace. If you can discern the fetal stirrings in the womb of the great Earth Mother, which obviously you can, and more crucially, if you can contemplate her capacity as great Birther and yet great Destroyer, and obviously you did that on December 26, 2004, then rightly we look to you as prophetic liberators for our time.

Go forth then and blaze that trail of promise and new hope! Governments and religions will ridicule you; evangelicals of every persuasion will condemn you; violent people will attack and try to harm you. They did it to me; they'll do it to you. But remember, I and the relational matrix are with you the whole way. So stand erect, hold your heads high, and deliver to my people the freedom they long have hungered for!

And next year on December 26, when you gather to cook fish for breakfast, count me in! We need to nourish and sustain each other for the difficult times ahead!

Yours Affectionately,

JOSHUA

Also from
Diarmuid O'Murchu

RELIGION IN EXILE
A Spiritual Homecoming

Diarmuid O'Murchu offers penetrating and original insights into the changing spiritual awareness of our time. He believes that we are rapidly out-growing the time honored but exhausted vision of formal religion.
0-8245-1841-1, $15.95, paperback

POVERTY, CELIBACY, AND OBEDIENCE
A Radical Option for Life

"A strong book, a daring call to relevance, a deep ground of religious life in humankind's holiest tradition."

—Barbara Fiand
0-8245-1473-4, $14.95 paperback

crossroad